YOU CAN
CHANGE
THE
WORLD

YOU CAN
CHANGE
THE
WORLD

Lars B. Dunberg

MOUNTAINBROOK
PRESS

You Can Change the World

By Lars B. Dunberg

Published by Mountainbrook Press,
5550 Tech Center Drive, Suite 302,
Colorado Springs, Colorado 80919
www.mountainbrookpress.com

ISBN 978-1-941113-64-6

Published in the United States by *Mountainbrook Press*

Cover design: Ron Adair

Interior Design: Jörgen Edelgård

Printed in the United States of America

2014 – First *Mountainbrook Press* Edition

Visit the *Mountainbrook Press* website from your mobile phone by scanning the code below.

iv

Contents

INTRODUCTION

"I can't!" "I don't dare!" "I don't have the strength." "That will cost too much!" "I don't know where to start!" Are these your usual defenses when people challenge you to be someone or get involved in something? It is one of the quickest reflexes we have.

Inherent to the culture in which I was raised, there is an underlying principle that no one should be better than anyone else. This is so rooted in the Scandinavian culture that it surprises me every time someone excels beyond the average. It is called the "Law of Jante," after a Danish-Norwegian novelist, Aksel Sandemose, who described an imaginary small town in Denmark called Jante. Having lived in a similar small town in Sweden, I know that nobody is anonymous – everyone knows everyone else – and their business!

Even today, the Law of Jante is commonly used in Scandinavia to poke fun at and negatively describe an attitude that aspires towards individuality and success.

The town of Jante had ten rules which could be summed up in the statement *"Don't think you're anyone special or that you're better than us."* The detailed rules went like this:

1. Don't think you're anything special
2. Don't think you're as good as us
3. Don't think you're smarter than us
4. Don't convince yourself that you're better than us
5. Don't think you know more than us
6. Don't think you are more important than us
7. Don't think you are good at anything
8. Don't laugh at us

9. Don't think anyone cares about you
10. Don't think you can teach us anything

I grew up in a home where the rules were shaped by an older cultural norm than the Law of Jante. My mother was the youngest of nine brothers and sisters. Her parents were born in 1859 and 1862 respectively. They came out of a culture where there was no real survival if you did not excel. My mother took that with her as she and my father started their family. Two aunts and four uncles, all born in the 19th century except one, ensured that their sister's children were raised in that same spirit.

As I grew up I realized that it did not matter how much I tried to excel, it was seldom good enough. This resulted in being driven by guilt in almost everything I did.

At the same time, it was always expected that I was able to do much more than I was doing — work better, study harder and certainly behave better. But I could not. Throughout my adult life, my mother was still in the background, and although they were seldom verbalized, I intuitively understood her expectations. She has been dead since 1993 but somehow my mother's expectations are still at times hanging over my head like some kind of guillotine, and I seem to be waiting for it to fall down on my head at any moment. All I could say as a young man was, "I can't do it!"

Before I married my fiancée I moved to England, where she lived. My English was still rather limited, and I struggled to express myself. I took the Jante attitude from home with me, but turned it inside out. What my future wife heard until she could not stand it anymore, was my literal translation of Swedish into English: "You must do this" and "you must do that" and "you have to behave in this way rather than that way!" Three weeks before the wedding she took me for a drive in her father's car and gave me a straight talking to. With tears running down her face, she exclaimed, "I can't stand it anymore! The wedding is off!" Praise God, she changed her mind a day later and now we have been married for 47 years!

INTRODUCTION

I can't! You must! These are not suitable expressions for anyone's vocabulary, and still we use them every day. However, when we open the Word of God, we notice how God uses ordinary people like you and me in the most impossible situations. For us, the most ordinary people living in impossible situations, he has tremendously strong words of encouragement.

In Philippians 4:13 we read, *For I can do everything through Christ, who gives me strength.*

Paul develops a similar thought in the book of Galatians. *My old self has been crucified with Christ. It is no longer I who live, but Christ lives in me. So I live in this earthly body by trusting in the Son of God, who loved me and gave himself for me (Gal 2:20).*

In 1 Corinthians 1:5 and 30, Paul explains why we can do all things through Jesus Christ. *Through him, God has enriched your church in every way — with all of your eloquent words and all of your knowledge…God has united you with Christ Jesus. For our benefit God made him to be wisdom itself. Christ made us right with God; he made us pure and holy, and he freed us from sin.*

He describes the blessings you and I can have in our lives. It does not need to be all negative. Life can be positive – but only through him. All praise to God, the Father of our Lord Jesus Christ, who has blessed us with every spiritual blessing in the heavenly realms because we are united with Christ. *Even before he made the world, God loved us and chose us in Christ to be holy and without fault in his eyes (Eph 1:4).*

Finally, in the Book of Colossians, Paul explains how we stay there. *Let your roots grow down into him, and let your lives be built on him. Then your faith will grow strong in the truth you were taught, and you will overflow with thankfulness (Col 2:7).*

God can. And through him, you can! That is what this book is all about.

CHAPTER ONE
YOU CAN get out of your misery

Meaninglessness and misery. Those words describe the lives of many people today. You may be one of them. You wake up and wonder how you are going to make it through yet another day. You are not necessarily physically ill. But your life is filled with misery that you have gathered up over the last days, weeks, months and years. Some of it has to do with other people being negative around you. They may have spoken or acted in ways that hurt deeply. You may have failed a test at school. After working two or three jobs you have either been laid off or fired. What a misery!

Or, perhaps over the years you have developed a lifestyle that may not be positive for your inner health. You may have become a slave to your own negative thoughts, or developed some compulsive addiction. Perhaps you gave in to impure thought patterns that developed into a fascination with pornography, and then blossomed out into a fairly regular promiscuous lifestyle. Maybe you have used drugs or excessive alcohol. Maybe it was something as simple as being so obsessed with your electronic toys or your job that all your personal relationships disappeared. A lot of that misery is simply self-inflicted.

You may also wonder what life is all about. If life is merely filled with guilt, or miserable experiences, broken relationships and never enough money for whatever you want to spend it on, and then ends abruptly at some point between the time you are born and around the average 70 years of age. Why continue living such a meaningless life?

YOU CAN

A few summers ago, my wife Doreen and I were in the province of Närke in Sweden, where my grandmother grew up. I was determined to see if I could find my great-grandfather's tomb stone. He had died in 1914. We visited a few church burial places around the small village where he had lived. After studying hundreds of tombstones surrounding three typical Swedish Lutheran churches, we gave up.

Sitting on a bench among all those grave stones, I turned to Doreen and philosophized, "If Sweden is looked upon as one of the most pagan and secular countries in the world, and most of the people who are lying here six feet underground believed that life ended the minute they died, then life must have been viewed as very miserable and meaningless to them."

If life only lasts 40-80 years, and meaning is found only in the experiences we have during those years, it would make sense to make "bucket lists" towards the end of your life to ensure you did not miss out on anything. You rush through life, hunting for experiences, and then it is simply over. Why bother to live out such meaninglessness in the first place?

On the other hand, some people find the meaning in life and live it to the fullest. Earlier in 2013, I participated in the funeral service of an old friend. When I first met him in 1979, Robert was 60 years old. He ran a nursery and sold fruit trees. He and his wife were so content — because in their early years they had found meaning in their lives though Jesus Christ. They dedicated their lives to raising four children as well as investing in the lives of thousands of people. They contributed to making the gospel heard around the world by giving the bulk of their income away. When Robert died he was 94, having worked basically every day of his adult life until he was 92.

I met Robert for the last time about six months before he died. I asked him what he thought when he looked back on his life. "I thank God that I could do a little to help other people," Robert said and continued, "God has been so good to me!" He had such a peace. No meaninglessness or misery there, even though he had been faced with his share of problems in life.

We cannot change our own situation. You and I can try to become a better person, but it is impossible. Our culture leads us to believe that we are, at our core, good people, but we are not, because while the culture has made us think we are "through-and-through" good people, we aren't. All of us have missed the mark. We can attempt to lift ourselves by our own bootstraps, and that helps for a little while, but what we really need is a complete change from the inside out.

My own story

I grew up in a Christian home in an extremely secular neighborhood in Stockholm, Sweden. I did not know of any child that had any Christian affiliation among my friends on my street or at school. I never wanted any of my friends to know about the religion of my parents. When friends came to our apartment to play, I ensured I had hidden everything religious in sight, from Bibles and religious pictures to hymn books.

Some of my aunts and both my grandmothers were also very solid believers. When I was ten years old, my grandmother, who by then was over ninety years old, came close to leaving her earthly life. I was over at her house with my mother; my grandmother, who was bedridden, asked me to come to her side. Suddenly she asked me to kneel down by her bed and as I did she placed her bony, old, wrinkly hands on my head and in her shaky voice muttered, "I am going to bless you." Then she prayed a prayer that I did not understand at all at that point in my life, but which has been etched into my memory ever since. "Lars, I bless you! You are going to preach to thousands of people across the world."

I reasoned with my ten-year-old mind that she did not know what she was talking about. My parents had never traveled anywhere outside Sweden with me, let alone gone to the other side of the world. Our vacations usually consisted of taking a bus and a boat to my dad's uncle's farm on one of the islands in the Stockholm archipelago. We did not have a car, and the only way my parents had traveled any distance was with an old tandem bicycle which, without fail, had a flat tire halfway towards their destination! And I hadn't met the Lord yet. Of course, long before that incident of my grandmother's blessing, we often played pretend church services at home. My sister and her dolls were forced to be the congregation. Sometimes my mother and father attended Lars' church as well. In one greatly inspired, tongue-twisted prayer, the young child-preacher wished that the Lord "would make all healthy people sick!" However, this was far from the reality I sensed in my grandmother's prayer.

The turning point

Then things went from bad to worse. A huge city-wide evangelistic crusade took place in Stockholm over a period of two months. Somehow I had a love-hate relationship with this crusade. I was fascinated by the dramatic preaching, the atmosphere as people walked forward to commit their lives to Christ, and the lively, inspiring music. But I also hated the public awareness this crusade was creating in my neighborhood. It made headline news in the secular press and most of the time the coverage was not very positive. People in general were talking about it, friends at school asked about it, and the kids on the street knew that somehow the "religious Dunbergs" had to be associated with it in one form or another.

Somehow I fought against the message that was preached every night. It was personal and radical and it cut into the bare bones of my 12-year old being. As we traveled home by streetcar every night, my parents would hint to me, "Lars, don't you think that this is the right time for you to commit your life to Christ?" My mother's eyes would well up with tears and her voice would tremble a bit, and I felt extremely awkward. The more they hinted, the more uncomfortable I became. I simply wanted to be left alone and sort out my faith on my own.

Finally, the next to last night of the crusade arrived. The old church where the services were being held had several levels of balconies, and I used to prefer to sit at the front row on the top one, peering down on the crowds on the main floor. Rev. Berthil Paulsson, Sweden's Billy Graham, was preaching that night, and I felt that his message was only for me. *He who comes to me I will certainly not throw out,* echoed the words through the massive church. That was not Reverend Paulsson speaking to me, it was Jesus!

Unbeknownst to my parents, I had been going out almost every night for the past few months with a gang of boys who liked to run around, knocking out the lights in the street lamps with sling shots. At times, we also enjoyed scaring old ladies by creeping up behind them, surprising them with sudden loud noises or screaming in their ears, watching the results when inevitably they would drop their handbags out of fright. We never stole anything; we just liked to scare them.

At other times, we would go down to the lake just a few minutes from my home. In the winter time we hopped about on the thin ice, jumping from one ice block to the other, finding our balance while the water seeped between the ice blocks. There were times when I would lose my balance and slip down between the ice blocks. It was a miracle I did not drown in the ice-cold water. I used to go to a friend's house, trying to dry my wet clothes on the radiators, and then sneak home, lying to my parents about what had happened. Jumping on the ice at the lake was absolutely forbidden territory. Suddenly, as I heard Jesus speaking to me, I realized I was the biggest sinner in the world. Was it true that Jesus would receive – even me?

When the invitation to receive Christ as your personal Savior was given, directly after the message, I could hardly wait to rush down to the front of the church. There the preacher would lead the people in the sinner's prayer, before the counselors would take over. They would then take the group to a private room, lead you through a prayer and then provide some basic information, as well as explain about a correspondence Bible study you would work through.

Unfortunately, in my eagerness to get down from the balcony, I took the wrong staircase. I opened the door in front of me, which I believed led to the main sanctuary of the church, but instead found myself out on the street! At that point it would have been easier to just go home, but I turned around, hurried through the right door and walked forward with many others. As Rev. Paulsson prayed the prayer for us to commit our lives to Jesus, I prayed with all the sincerity of a twelve-year-old's heart. In the counseling room, I struggled through the first sheet of the correspondence Bible course, designed by the Navigators. It was not very user-friendly for my age group, and I felt very embarrassed that I did not quite understand all the questions. I was already six foot three and people thought I was much older. However, that night, my grandmother's blessing and prayer made sense for the first time in my life.

Out of misery – into a joyful life

People have used many phrases to describe the process of turning from misery to joy. The Bible sometimes calls it salvation. Some call it "the new birth." Others speak about it as "a beam of light into a dark room," and still others talk about it as the core element of the Good News which Jesus brought into the world.

The term salvation can be difficult to understand. It is one of those strange words you often hear in church. But what does it mean? Salvation is a key word in the Bible, where it is mentioned over 286 times. Before we go into all the details, let me make three statements from my own experience.

Salvation is something you can experience, not just after death, but right now.
Paul writes in his letters in the New Testament, *But because of his great love for us, God, who is rich in mercy, made us alive with Christ even when we were dead in transgressions – it is by grace you have been saved* (Eph 2:4-5).

For he has rescued us from the dominion of darkness and brought us into the kingdom of the Son he loves (Col 1:13).

He saved us, not because of righteous things we had done, but because of his mercy. He saved us through the washing of rebirth and renewal by the Holy Spirit (Titus 3:5-6).

God's way of saving is simple and straightforward.

As I told you, when I was twelve years old God came into my life. He transformed me completely and gave me peace, joy and a new life. I did not know any theology or deep spiritual truths, but what I needed to know as a young man I found out. I heard Jesus say from the New Testament, *He that comes to me I shall never cast out.* I came to him and found the statement was true. It is straightforward.

Salvation is also a fantastic mystery.

When I was saved, it was not only a moral transformation inside my heart, but it began a process that was reflected in my life. It was as if Jesus had made a supernatural entry of peace, life, and love into my personality. God began a transformation within me, from the inside out, which is still going on today.

The word "salvation"

The word *salvation* is not specifically a Christian word, because there are several religions that talk about salvation. However, their understanding of salvation differs from the understanding we get from the Bible. For example, the Muslims think of salvation as a paradise where all spiritual and bodily desires are fulfilled. The Hindus see salvation as liberation from a cycle of rebirth to an expanded outlook, while for Buddhists salvation is reaching Nirvana, which is a transcendental, blissful, spiritual state of nothingness where you become a Buddha. Marxists see salvation as the reconstruction of society in such a way as to make it the basis for man's true return to himself. In general, people see that things are not as they should be and inherently feel the need for salvation. In this book we will learn the basic things about salvation from a Christian perspective.

The word salvation means "to preserve or rescue from natural dangers." In the New Testament, it is used to describe deliverance from acute danger, like the time when the disciples were almost sinking in the storm at sea, and Jesus saved them by calming the storm. But the most common use of the word salvation in the New Testament is to describe freedom from sin. *You are to name him Jesus, for he will save his people from their sins* (Matt 1:21). The apostle Paul says in 1 Timothy 1:15 that *Christ Jesus came into the world to save sinners.*

Christian salvation deals with the root problem of the human heart: sin. Christian salvation is a gift from God, and it is totally free. We don't need to achieve salvation by doing a lot of good things, or by performing religious rites — as is invariably the case in all other religions.

Instead of trying to climb up to God, he has come down to us! He became what we are, so that we can become what he is. *For God made Christ, who never sinned, to be the offering for our sin, so that we could be made right with God through Christ* (2 Corinthians 5:21).

The foundation and meaning of salvation

The foundation of salvation is the life, death and resurrection of Jesus Christ. The cross is crucial for salvation, but without the resurrection, the cross would have no meaning. The meaning of the death of Jesus Christ is shown to us in the New Testament by way of many different images. We are going to look at some of these now.

Salvation is simply God's way of providing deliverance for his people from sin and spiritual death. It happens through repentance and faith in Jesus Christ. The New Testament reveals that the source of salvation is found in Jesus Christ. By believing in Jesus Christ, people are saved from God's judgment of sin and its consequence — eternal death.

Ephesians 1:7 tells us, *He is so rich in kindness and grace that he purchased our freedom with the blood of his Son and forgave our sins.*

We were all prisoners of sin. You as well as I. In the Book of John, Jesus says, *That is why I said that you will die in your sins; for unless you believe that I AM WHO I CLAIM TO BE, YOU WILL DIE IN YOUR SINS.* The same concept is underscored by Romans 3:23. *For everyone has sinned; we all fall short of God's glorious standard.*

We are all sinners in the eyes of the Lord — even if we have different appearances. Some wear beautiful, expensive clothes; others are dressed in dirty rags that have worn thin after being worn for a long time. Some are heard swearing while others are uttering pious phrases. Some live in palaces while others are sleeping under a tarp, held up by two sticks. Some are religious prisoners and some are atheistic prisoners, but they are all prisoners.

What do I mean by calling them prisoners? The Book of Ephesians states, *Once you were dead because of your disobedience and your many sins. You used to live in sin, just like the rest of the world, obeying the devil — the commander of the powers in the unseen world. He is the spirit at work in the hearts of those who refuse to obey God. All of us used to live that way, following the passionate desires and inclinations of our sinful nature. By our very nature we were subject to God's anger, just like everyone else* (Eph 2:1-3).

We can try to be different, but it does not help. We can attempt to better ourselves, but it is of no use. God wants to have an intimate relationship with us, but we cannot obtain it through our own efforts. Isaiah 64:6, *All of us have become like one who is unclean, and all our righteous acts are like filthy rags.* Rom 3:10-12 echoes the same: *There is no one righteous, not even one; there is no one who understands, no one who seeks God. All have turned away, they have together become worthless; there is no one who does good, not even one.* We are all prisoners under the grip of sin.

Imagine a transport of prisoners, walking along the road. They are bound to each other by shackles, both to their hands and feet. They are weary, bent over and dirty.

Suddenly someone lifts his hands, as the shackles have fallen off. He shouts, "Hallelujah, I have been set free. I was bound by bad habits and under the influence of drugs. But Jesus just came by and he set me free!"

A young lady, just behind him, raises her hands, completely unshackled. "Hallelujah, I am also free! I used to hate my parents and my family. I could not stand them. I ran away from home and lived in bitterness, hate and misery. But Jesus has changed my heart and I am set free. Now I can love my parents!"

The word salvation means that you have been unshackled from your own personal chains of sin and have been set free by the power of the blood of Jesus.

The Bible indicates that we need this experience of God if life is to be lived with dynamism and purpose. Without God we find no satisfying alternative way of life.

We have freedom through his blood.

Why blood?

In the time of the Mao Revolution in the Republic of China, the young people in Mao uniforms, waving Mao Zedong's little Red Book, used to shout, "Without blood there is no revolution." In the Scriptures we find there is no transformation from the power of bondage without the sacrifice of blood. When Adam and Eve realized they were naked, an animal had to die and sacrifice its blood, so the animal's hide could be made into clothes for our first parents. When the children of Israel were ready to flee their captivity in Egypt, they were instructed to kill a lamb and paint the blood of that lamb on their door posts. The blood of the slaughtered lamb protected the people from the angel of death.

As we can see in the laws that were written during Israel's long walk through the wilderness, many of the offerings described involved the sacrifice of animals for the sake of sin, with their blood sprinkled on the altar.

Today, God the Father looks upon the blood of his son. That is the sacrifice for the cleansing of sinners like you and me. When he sees that blood, he will forgive us and transform us. Not when he sees your tears, or your goodness, or that you are better than your neighbor, or that you married a Christian partner. It is the blood that cleanses from all sin. *But if we are living in the light, as God is in the light, then we have fellowship with each other, and the blood of Jesus, his Son, cleanses us from all sin* (1 John 1:7).

Why do we have a cross as a piece of jewellery round our necks? Why are there crosses in Christian churches? Why is there often a cross on the communion table? These things remind us of the blood of Jesus.

I remember when the first heart transplant took place in 1967, by Dr. Christian Barnard, a South African surgeon. As we followed the news, we learned that the success of the operation did not just depend on the surgeon. The patient could either reject the new heart and die, or assimilate it into the body system and survive. Jesus Christ is both the donor and the surgeon. He has given his life, his heart so to speak, to give us eternal life. He did this on the cross. He is willing to place his life in us and give us his nature. But while he is willing to give us a new heart and cleanse us in his blood, we, the patients, can either reject him or accept him. One leads to death and the other one leads to life.

So, Jesus is not just some kind of religious ambulance that comes to us when we feel things are falling apart, applying some bandages here and there where we feel they are needed. No, he is the heart surgeon, placing us on the operating table and offers us a complete transformation into a new being. The apostle Paul describes it like this: *This means that anyone who belongs to Christ has become a new person. The old life is gone; a new life has begun!* (2 Cor 5:17)

This move of God includes forgiveness of sins. The reminder of sins in our life is the feeling we normally call guilt. While the post-modern world denies that guilt exists, it lives in every human being. Here are some dictionary definitions of the word guilt: "Guilt is an emotion that occurs when a person believes that they have violated a moral standard that they themselves believe in," or "responsibility for a crime or for doing something bad or wrong" or "a bad feeling caused by knowing or thinking that you have done something bad or wrong."

According to the Scriptures, God has recorded every part of our lives in his book. It is as if he has made a DVD of our lives and one day it will play out in front of everyone, our thoughts, our words — even our actions. That is why forgiveness is so fantastic! God in his goodness, through the power of the blood of Jesus, wipes the slate clean. *I — yes, I alone — will blot out your sins for my own sake and will never think of them again* (Isa 43:25).

As the well-known Dutch Concentration Camp survivor Corrie ten Boom used to say, "But the joy is that Corrie Ten Boom knew what to do with her sins. When I confessed them to the Father, Jesus Christ washed them in his blood. They are now cast into the deepest sea and a sign is put up that says, NO FISHING ALLOWED!"

One of the most intriguing conversion stories I have ever witnessed took place in one of the churches in Newcastle, England. One Sunday night I had been invited to speak in this rather large church, and even on a Sunday night the church was almost packed. That night I preached on the power in the word "salvation" and the fact that the blood of Jesus can cleanse us from all sin. As I gave the invitation for people to come forward to receive Christ, one man stood up at the back of the church. But instead of moving to the area in front of me, where others were gathering to commit their lives to Christ, he walked straight passed me, opened the door and stepped into the pastor's vestry that was situated behind the pulpit. I handed the service back over to the pastor and followed the man into the vestry. Immediately the man grabbed hold of my jacket lapels and put his angry face up close to mine. "Who told you about me," he hissed through his clenched teeth, "How do you know everything about me?" I knew nothing of this man! Later, a few people from the audience told me that this fellow was their co-worker. Every Sunday night he would come to the service, not to be blessed, but to observe everything, so he could make fun of the church, the pastor, Christians and the Christian faith on Monday, when they all returned to work. "He used to be like a devil on Mondays," they exclaimed. Now he stood here before me.

"Is it true what you told me? That there is forgiveness for me?" Then he began to tell me his story, as later confirmed by his workmates. I told him that he could be forgiven. "But you haven't heard it all," he continued, and then spewed out a life of moral decay, incestuous living and behavior that was more than I had faced from anyone else ever before. "Is there really forgiveness for me?" he cried out as he fell to the floor.

"The blood of Jesus Christ cleanses from all sin," I quickly replied.

Then, there followed a wrestling match in prayer the likes of which I have hardly ever experienced since. Darkness so completely surrounded this man as he tried to confess and ask for forgiveness and cleansing that as I watched him, I was not sure what was going to happen. And then, in a flash, the atmosphere changed. It was like lights had been turned on everywhere in the pastor's study as the man rose, with his face shining. "What has happened to me?" he asked as tears were streaming down his face, "I have not cried like this since I was a little boy!" God's forgiveness and transformation had suddenly set in with an electrifying force I had seldom observed, and I realized again the enormous power in the cleansing blood of Jesus.

Only Jesus can change our spiritual misery. *When God our Savior revealed his kindness and love, he saved us, not because of the righteous things we had done, but because of his mercy. He washed away our sins, giving us a new birth and new life through the Holy Spirit* (Titus 3:4-5).

Today you can be free from your misery and live out a life in complete freedom with God.

CHAPTER TWO
YOU CAN bleed the right color

The driver of the van in front of me on Interstate 25 slammed on his breaks as I was driving to the Denver airport to catch a morning flight. There had been an accident ahead of me and the road quickly turned into a parking lot. The only thing left to do was to study the stickers on the rear door of the van in front of me. The whole door was covered with stickers, and suddenly I noticed they were all orange in support of the Denver football team, the Broncos. One in particular that caught my interest simply said, "If you scratch me, I bleed orange."

What color do you bleed if I scratch you?

When I was a young Salvationist we often took part in meetings where testimonies were given. The favorite color of The Salvation Army's members was, and still is, the color red; a reminder of the blood of Jesus Christ. The most common testimonies given by my friends went something like this, "I don't want to be like a radish; red on the outside while colorless and hard on the inside. I want to be like a tomato; soft and red all throughout!"

What color do you bleed if I scratch you a little?

Passionate followers

What are you passionate about? What makes you laugh or cry? Is it your political involvement? Is it the economy? Is it your iPhone, or iPad? Or is it the possibility of becoming a true follower of Jesus Christ?

There weren't many Jesus followers in the days when he walked here on earth. Most of the people surrounding Jesus were enthusiastic admirers. Some of them were almost fanatics. I may have been one of them if I lived in those days. They received free food when he fed 5,000 people, with the help of only five loaves and two fish. They saw miracles when he walked on the water and when he healed the sick. They wanted to be very close to him. They were truly enthusiastic Jesus admirers.

My son Paul is an ice hockey enthusiast. When it comes to the Denver ice-hockey team called The Avalanche, he is more or less a fanatic. He watches every game: most times on TV, but preferably in person — whenever he can afford it. One time he brought his mom and dad along! We sat properly outfitted in ice hockey jerseys right behind one of the goals.

I noticed the people were very excited. Some had painted their faces with the colors of their favorite team. Others proudly waved scarves bearing the colors of their team. They shouted and clapped frenetically. But not one of them had ever been part of the team. They had never been tackled on the ice. No one ever had a puck shot in their face and as a result lost their front teeth. They had never pushed themselves beyond what they thought they could accomplish physically, to score a goal. They were simply spectators.

These fans seem to know everything about the players. They can tell you all the statistics about every possible play. Yet they don't know any of the players personally. And they certainly don't know the team captain. They shout and scream, but they never expect to do anything beyond that. No sacrifice is needed because their role is to be spectators only. They are enthusiasts, but not participants or followers. Jesus has many enthusiasts. You may be one of them. You know every story about him. You can describe in great detail what he did 2,000 years ago. But can he do something in your life now? Will you be his follower?

Some of us repeat the Lord's Prayer over and over, or we may have raised our hand to receive Jesus at a summer camp or an evangelistic meeting some thirty years ago. Some make a decision for Jesus, but there is not enough conviction to become a follower.

When we read the four Gospels we notice that five times Jesus says, "Believe in me." However, about twenty times he says, "Follow me." One is not more important than the other. But they cannot exclude each other.

Over the past 35 years, I have had the opportunity to work in almost every area of India. Many of the believers have been harassed for their faith by relatives, friends or even complete strangers. Every week I receive email messages via the *Evangelical Fellowship of India* about Christians being persecuted and physically abused for their faith.

One day in 2013, in the state of Chhattisgarh, Hindu extremists allegedly disrupted a prayer meeting and later beat a Christian unconscious. The incident took place when five people barged into the prayer meeting of a house church. One believer told the extremists to leave the place and not to disturb them again. The angry extremists dragged that believer to a field and beat him up with thorny sticks. Thereafter they took him to a house where they hit him on his head with a plowhead. The man fell unconscious after the blow. The church members found their "believer brother" on the road in a semi-conscious state. He suffered a deep cut on his head, bruises and abrasions all over his body.

In a city in northeast India, a Christian was brutally murdered after he refused to renounce Christ. The beheaded body of this brother was found in a stream, reported the newsletter.

In southern India, Hindu extremists beat up a Christian widow and left her unconscious on the road. Her daughter, who was with her mother, was also hurt. The extremists barged into the widow's house and questioned her about her faith. They later dragged her and her daughter to the local Hindu temple and tried to forcefully convert them back into Hinduism. However, both women firmly refused to denounce Christ. Then the extremists slapped, kicked and punched them for almost an hour until the widow fell to the ground, unconscious. The two Christians were hospitalized for three days.

Ram Swaroop Majhi turned 41 in 2013. He and his wife Emil live in the state of Jharkhand in India. Ram was born in a Hindu family, but came to know Jesus Christ through an evangelist who led him to the Lord. After accepting Jesus he faced many problems from his family and the local villagers. To make him suffer, they broke his hands. But Ram continued to be a witness for Jesus Christ, despite suffering such pain. Today he is working in a Christian hospital, where he also takes time to counsel the patients.

These people are not just enthusiasts for Jesus. They are his followers. They bleed for Jesus, some of them literally.

What are you doing? In his book *Not a Fan*, Kyle Idleman writes,

"Most of us don't mind Jesus making some minor changes in our lives, but Jesus wants to turn our lives upside down. Fans don't mind him doing a little touch-up work, but Jesus wants complete renovation. Fans come to Jesus thinking tune-up, but Jesus is thinking makeover. Fans think a little decorating is required, but Jesus wants a complete remodel. Fans want Jesus to inspire them, but Jesus wants to interfere with their lives."

Kyle Idleman continues to tell the story of Nicodemus, who came to Jesus at night. Nicodemus had spent his whole adult life building a religious resume, but Jesus made clear that those standards did not apply. Nicodemus would have to be born again. It was not enough that Nicodemus believed that Jesus had come from God. Jesus wanted Nicodemus to become a follower, not just at night, but during the day as well.

How was it when you came to Christ? You knew you needed to make a commitment somewhere along your life journey, and it was underlined by the need to believe in Jesus Christ. But did you ever hear clearly that you also need to follow him? Bleed a little red?

Idleman continues to tell a story about a man who came up to him after he had preached in a church in Texas. The man described how their daughter had gone to college and completely turned her back on her faith. At the end of his monologue, he didn't ask what she had done wrong or why she was behaving in this way. He simply stated, "We raised her in Church, but we didn't raise her in Christ!"

During my years of ministry I have worked in areas where Christianity was basically forbidden. To lead someone to Christ was not impossible, but the price these believers had to pay for their new faith was sometimes beyond comprehension. In 1977, Ken Taylor, the man behind the *Living Bible,* and I, were in a Middle-Eastern country together, meeting with a Bible translator. When we finally located him at the university compound where he worked, he looked very troubled, closed the door and drew the blinds. "I worked on the manuscript at home, but my wife found it and burned it. So now I come over here early in the morning and work on a new manuscript. With God's help I will continue." Fearing for his life, he continued to stand up for his faith.

One of the first translation projects I became involved in as the Director of *Living Bibles International* in Europe in the 70's, was translating the Scripture into the Czech language. This was during some of the darkest days of Communist oppression. There was intense pressure on Christians. Publishing Scripture was prohibited, but several church leaders wanted to get a contemporary translation underway. A translation team was formed, but they lived in different parts of the country and could not communicate easily. Telephones were tapped. Letters could be opened and read by Communist Party officials. One member of the team had been given a suspended sentence for previous Christian activity, and if he were to be caught working in this way again, he would have been imprisoned immediately. So the translation work continued clandestinely. It was imperative for the team to meet, but it had to be arranged with maximum security.

Meetings of Christians in many parts of Eastern Europe were hazardous affairs in those days. Those who were attending needed to be sure they were not being followed. Conversations were conducted in whispers, especially in apartments with thin walls! Pillows were put over telephones because conversations within the room could be monitored even though the phone was firmly on the hook. Any noise, such as footsteps outside the apartment, was treated with suspicion.

Meeting with foreigners was forbidden, so if the Secret Police became aware of any such contact, the person concerned was subject to intense interrogation.

Long before personal computers were invented, manuscripts were typed with several carbon copies so that, if any were discovered by the authorities, all would not be lost. Photocopiers were unavailable, and any kinds of writing equipment, even typewriters, were supposed to be registered with the authorities.

On the rare occasions when we could meet with the team, the atmosphere was fraught with tension. When we were close to the venue, we would circle the block and then walk back and forth to ensure we were not being followed. But all this was worth it, simply to spend time with the team and to be in the presence of some very special servants of God. They were willing to bleed red to ensure their country could understand the Word of God.

In the past few years there has been no end of turmoil, especially for Christians in the country of Egypt. A friend of mine is the senior pastor of a huge church in Cairo. Prior to that, he was a physician and used to serve as my interpreter when I preached at his church. Attending a pastors' conference in 2013 in San Diego, I found, to my surprise, that he was the final presenter. He challenged us in many ways to "bleed red." One of the most touching stories he told was about a Muslim leader who had come to faith in Christ and was being added to the church.

At the baptismal service, one of the elders, who was going to baptize this former Muslim leader, asked him,

"Are you ready for this?"

"For what?" he replied.

"You may be killed if you are baptized; are you ready for this?"

The former Muslim answered,

"Did you see Jesus?"

"Well, not really," the elder said. "Yes by faith, but not face to face."

"You don't know how much you are missing! If you had seen Jesus, you would not have asked me such a question. I am ready to die for him."

You can bleed red. Stand up for your faith. Become a Jesus follower. *I can do all things through him who gives me strength* (Phil 4:13).

CHAPTER THREE
YOU CAN win the impossible battle

Somehow what's in our hearts, good or bad, is eventually translated into words and deeds. That's a bit scary.

Andy Stanley

Holiness is not a program to improve our lives but rather God's
transforming power working deep in our hearts.

John Wimber

I was in one of my favorite breakfast places the other week. They
have the most delicious omelets! On the table was a stand with
some advertising for their most sumptuous dishes and the slogan
simply stated, "Temptation is not always bad!" I have to disagree.
Every temptation that comes our way will lead to us either giving
in to it, or resisting it. To most of us it seems to be an impossible
battle. As we give in to what we think is a good temptation, ratio-
nalizing each step as appropriate and normal, we soon find that
the temptation has snared us in a cycle of self-justification that we
cannot break out of. Is there a way to win this impossible battle?

What temptation is not

What is it we are tempted to do? Before we go there, let me be
clear: a lot of things some of us once thought were horrible sins,
things that we were tempted to do, were simply cultural — behavior demanded by the church in an attempt to teach us goodness, or
to protect us from harm.

I grew up in an old, cultural, traditional family, where everything that was not considered "Christian" was wrong. We were allowed to watch slide pictures on the screen, but not if the pictures moved. Movies were things we were not even to think about. It was definitely sinful to go to the cinema or the theatre, and any form of dance was viewed as nothing but African pre-sexual rites. Card games were obvious tools in the devil's hand. When school dances were held, I had a note from home for my teacher informing her that I did not dance. When it was time to go and see a movie with the school, I was excused.

Earrings and make-up were not introduced into evangelical church circles until the 50s, and my small ears pricked up when I heard my mother disapprovingly describe what some of the ladies in church had started wearing. When one of my parents' best lady-friends came for a visit, and I opened the door, she must have had a shock for I simply left her standing there, and running into my mother, I literally cried, "Mummy, Auntie Karin will not go to heaven! She has earrings!"

When I was ten years old, Billy Graham came to town. Every newspaper carried photos of Billy and his wife Ruth. When my mother saw those pictures, she simply stated, "She can't be a believer. She wears earrings and make-up."

My mother taught classical piano to students in our home, and she often also played classical music herself. Therefore I was rather taken aback by her reaction when I had saved up enough money to buy my first "Long Playing" record. I was fourteen, and one day I took my savings, went to the music store and bought Haydn's Trumpet Concerto. Upon returning home, I happily showed it to my mother, who then immediately turned around and went into the kitchen, crying. After a while, she came back to me with tears streaming down her face and said, "Will this music lead you into other interests than the Lord?"

This worry and concern never left her. Many years later, when Doreen and I had been married some 20 years and lived in Chicago, my staff gave us theatre tickets for *The Nutcracker Suite* at

Christmas. As we called my parents to wish them a Merry Christmas, I shared the news about this great gift with her. She went quiet, and then responded, "How can you, as a Christian leader, go to the theatre, even taking your entire family?"

The Lord had to continually work on freeing me from a lot of these lists of "don'ts." Today, I am more than troubled over the legalism in these behavioral patterns. At the same time, there are some aspects of pietistic behavior that I miss in present day church life. It did set Christians apart from the world in a very visible form and created a modesty that would not hurt today's modern society. Some of the taboos, for which there was no great rhyme or reason, and from which I am freed today, still tend to create emotional tugs within me. Even now I feel uncomfortable when I see a deck of cards and although my children have had decks of cards, and make fun of their father, they know that it is impossible to persuade me to play any kind of card game.

A lot of these issues which we mistake for sin are simply a misguided understanding of culture. Traveling the world I soon realized that every culture has its own lists of so-called "sins" by which you can be tempted.

In some countries, you can witness people who are offended by Christians who drink a beer or wine uttering their complaints through lips that are holding a cigar in place! In some parts of Russia, you cannot preach wearing a tie because the tie points to hell! In some churches in the state of Kerala, India, you cannot preach in a short sleeve shirt, because it exposes your arms. However, the people who are most adamant about condemning these shirts, wear their *dhoti* (or lower body garment) wrapped around their legs lifted over their knees, and when they sit on a stage you can see right up their legs! That is somehow more spiritual than showing a bare forearm! Go figure! It is nothing but culture.

What is it we are tempted to do?

At the same time, Scripture talks about temptations to sin in areas that have very little to do with culture, and those are the temptations we need to overcome. As believers we struggle with life and behavior. We want to be like Jesus, but our work and life often take us to situations and places where we are tempted. The enemy is after all of us. We often feel lonely and assume that we cannot share our struggles and temptations with others. I find that most of the counseling I do deals with temptation and defeat of the inner life. It can be bad habits or the destructive power of drugs. It can be wild fantasies that later turn into reality. The most common problem among pastors in the Western world is the grip of pornography. Pornography has become such an epidemic that not only families, but lifelong ministries are destroyed by it. And today, laymen as well as pastors seem to be snared by pornography more than ever. The guilt is enormous. The depression goes deep and the disappointment is huge.

Almost every week I hear about some new pastor having problems with the key areas of Satan's attacks. When pastors meet, we ask: what are the greatest temptations in ministry? And it seems that the greatest temptations are sex, money, and power.

The Book of Proverbs, Chapter 5, describes men who are tempted by an adulterous relationship. Chapter 5:8 spells out a way to avoid temptation. *Keep to a path far from her. Do not go near the door of her house!*

The grandmother of spiritual death

How can we win these kinds of battles? The first lesson is not to go to the areas where the temptation lives. It draws us strongly. We have to stand against it. James, in his first chapter, describes what I call "The grandmother of spiritual death." He clearly points out that we are the ones who take the first step, which in turn drags us beyond temptation to actions that ultimately lead to spiritual death.

God blesses those who patiently endure testing and temptation. Afterward they will receive the crown of life that God has promised to those who love him. And remember, when you are being tempted, do not say, "God is tempting me." God is never tempted to do wrong, and he never tempts anyone else. Temptation comes from our own desires, which entice us and drag us away. These desires give birth to sinful actions. And when sin is allowed to grow, it gives birth to death (Jas 1:12-15).

Tempting, tempting

We cannot face every temptation on our own, and then wonder why we fail. In one church, a teenager in the youth group became pregnant. Talking to the youth pastor, she blurted out, "I don't understand how it happened! We prayed before every date!" The youth director just looked at her and asked, "What'd you do after you prayed?" The only way to overcome temptation is to look at Jesus Christ. We have to stop looking at what tempts us and look at Jesus instead.

Paul said, *The temptations in your life are no different from what others experience. And God is faithful. He will not allow the temptation to be more than you can stand. When you are tempted, he will show you a way out so that you can endure* (1 Cor 10:13).

Temptations come in many forms and shapes. We tend to scale sins as well as temptations to sin. One friend of mine, who was accused of a homosexual act while in ministry, told me, "Some people would have considered it not so bad if it had been a woman!" The people who gossip about these "shocking" sins, and condemn others, have fallen for a different kind of temptation — but with the same end result: spiritual death.

What are you tempted by today? Eating too much? Exercising so much that you have no time for God? Buying things you don't really need? Badly mistreating the people around you? The temptation to give in to anger is huge in many of us.

Several years ago, I was diagnosed with an incurable disease. The only thing that would help me would be to take huge doses of steroids intermittently for the rest of my life. So, I started taking the doses for a few months. It changed my personality drastically, and lowered my will power against temptation like I could never have imagined. Walking into a store, I had a horrendous urge to shoplift. Sexual temptations that had previously been dormant flared up in such a way that I had to make a choice — to stay on the medication or to get out of Christian ministry and simply give in. I have not been on steroids since! I learned, however, what real temptations are like, and I understand that there are times when it seems impossible to overcome them.

Tempted by chocolate? I am — often. Even when the result of giving in could easily be a migraine the next day! Attracted to someone other than your spouse? That is one of the most common downfalls for friends, co-workers or people in ministry, regardless of geography. Like getting drunk or using illicit drugs? Temptations are all around us. In the state of Colorado, where I live, marijuana is now the legal drug for an extra kick. What a temptation!

What sets your temptation off? Those are the moments, places and thought patterns to move away from. Can you resist temptation, and make these correct choices, by yourself? No. However hard you try, it will not work for long. There is only one permanent solution.

In 1957, Bible expositor Donald Grey Barnhouse (1895-1960), preached a sermon entitled *Temptation and How to Meet It* in which he offers three ways to defeat temptation. He ended his sermon with this summary statement:

"You're going to be tempted by the flesh. Run away. You're going to be tempted by the devil. Stand up and fight with the Word of God in your hand, the sword of the Spirit, and the shield of faith wherewith you shall be able to quench all the fiery darts of the evil one (Eph 6:16). And as to the world round about you, be not conformed, but day by day, ask God to pour you into the mold of Christ."

Temptation is a very common problem for all of us. Victory over temptation is not so common. The problem is that we entertain ourselves by looking at the temptation rather than staring into the solution —Jesus Christ.

On the night Christ was betrayed, he told his disciples in the garden: *Keep watching and praying that you may not enter into temptation; the spirit is willing, but the flesh is weak* (Matt 26:41). We do not openly want to jump into sin, yet we cannot resist falling into it because our flesh is not strong enough to resist. We need to renew our thinking. *And so, dear brothers and sisters, I plead with you to give your bodies to God because of all he has done for you. Let them be a living and holy sacrifice — the kind he will find acceptable. This is truly the way to worship him. Don't copy the behavior and customs of this world, but let God transform you into a new person by changing the way you think. Then you will learn to know God's will for you, which is good and pleasing and perfect* (Rom 12:1-2).

Proverbs 4:14-15 tells us: *don't do as the wicked do and don't follow the path of evildoers. Don't even think about it; don't go that way. Turn away and keep moving.*

You can win this impossible battle. The Bible tells us we can become "overcomers," or as more modern translations say it, *victorious.* It is mentioned several times in the Book of Revelation.

We overcome the enemy by following Christ, and by letting him successfully resist the power and temptation of the world's system in our lives. It does not mean we become sinless, but we hold on to our faith in Christ until the end. We depend on God for his direction, purpose, fulfillment, and we lean on his strength in our lives.

Overcoming temptation begins with standing firm and refusing to be dragged into it. James 4:7 says, *Resist the devil and he will flee from you.* In chapter 8 of Romans, Paul encourages us by stating in verse 37, *In all these things we are more than conquerors through him who loved us.*

Here are the promises for the victorious ones, taken from the Book of Revelation. Jesus says they:

- Eat from the Tree of Life (Rev 2:7).
- Be unharmed by the second death (Rev 2:11).
- Eat hidden manna and be given a new name (Rev 2:17).
- Have authority over the nations (Rev 2:26).

- Be clothed in white garments (Rev 3:5).
- Be made permanent pillars in the House of God (Rev 3:12).
- Sit with Jesus on his throne (Rev 3:21).

Jesus, as a man, a human, endured every temptation that can ever come across any person's way, and he faced temptation just as we have to face it. Hebrews 4:15 makes that clear when it says, *but we have a High Priest who has been tempted in every way, just as we are – yet was without sin.* In the time of temptation, Jesus exercised the same power that is offered to us by God today.

Galatians 5 tells us that as we are filled with his Spirit, the fruit of the Spirit becomes noticeable in our lives. It seems that the fruit of the Spirit is nothing but a display of the character of Jesus. Through his faithfulness we can show his character. What he wants to tell us through his holy life is that we can walk as he walked.

> *Therefore, since Christ suffered in his body, arm yourselves also with the same attitude, because he who has suffered in his body is done with sin. As a result, he does not live the rest of his earthly life for evil human desires, but rather for the will of God* (1 Peter 4:1-2).

Jesus wants us to live his holy life, as we let him take ownership of our lives. We flee temptation through the power of Jesus living within us. *Make every effort to live in peace with all men and to be holy; without holiness no one will see the Lord. See to it that no one misses the grace of God and that no bitter root grows up to cause trouble and defile many. See that no one is sexually immoral, or is godless like Esau, who for a single meal sold his inheritance rights as the oldest son* (Heb 12:14-16).

Only a new call to that kind of holy living will set this generation free.

It is only Jesus who can help us through daily temptations. We can reason through them, hide them, talk ourselves out of them, but it is only Jesus who can set us free. It is he that equips us to be able to stand against all temptation. Here are some Scriptures to remind you of your temptation and what he does to lead you out of such situations.

And remember, when you are being tempted, do not say, 'God is tempting me.' God is never tempted to do wrong, and he never tempts anyone else (Jas 1:13).

The temptations in your life are no different from what others experience. And God is faithful. He will not allow the temptation to be more than you can stand. When you are tempted, he will show you a way out so that you can endure (1 Cor 10:13).

Run from sexual sin! No other sin so clearly affects the body as this one does. For sexual immorality is a sin against your own body. Don't you realize that your body is the temple of the Holy Spirit, who lives in you and was given to you by God? You do not belong to yourself, for God bought you with a high price. So you must honor God with your body (1 Cor 6:18-20).

Remember, it is sin to know what you ought to do and then not do it (Jas 4:17).

So humble yourselves before God. Resist the devil, and he will flee from you (Jas 4:7).

So I say, let the Holy Spirit guide your lives. Then you won't be doing what your sinful nature craves (Gal 5:16).

This High Priest of ours understands our weaknesses, for he faced all of the same testings we do, yet he did not sin (Heb 4:15). *My dear children, I am writing this to you so that you will not sin. But if anyone does sin, we have an advocate who pleads our case before the Father. He is Jesus Christ, the one who is truly righteous* (1 John 2:1).

There he told them, 'Pray that you will not give in to temptation' (Luke 22:40).

And don't let us yield to temptation, but rescue us from the evil one (Matt 6:13).

If we claim we have no sin, we are only fooling ourselves and not living in the truth (1 John 1:8).

Stay alert! Watch out for your great enemy, the devil. He prowls around like a roaring lion, looking for someone to devour. Stand firm against him, and be strong in your faith. Remember that your Christian brothers and sisters all over the world are going through the same kind of suffering you are.

In his kindness God called you to share in his eternal glory by means of Christ Jesus. So after you have suffered a little while, he will restore, support, and strengthen you, and he will place you on a firm foundation. All power to him forever! Amen (1 Pet 5:8-11).

Dear friends, don't be surprised at the fiery trials you are going through, as if something strange were happening to you. Instead, be very glad — for these trials make you partners with Christ in his suffering, so that you will have the wonderful joy of seeing his glory when it is revealed to all the world (1 Pet 4:12-13).

Since he himself has gone through suffering and testing, he is able to help us when we are being tested (Heb 2:18).

God blesses those who patiently endure testing and temptation. Afterward they will receive the crown of life that God has promised to those who love him (Jas 1:12).

A final word: Be strong in the Lord and in his mighty power. Put on all of God's armor so that you will be able to stand firm against all strategies of the devil. For we are not fighting against flesh-and-blood enemies, but against evil rulers and authorities of the unseen world, against mighty powers in this dark world, and against evil spirits in the heavenly places.

Therefore, put on every piece of God's armor so you will be able to resist the enemy in the time of evil. Then after the battle you will still be standing firm. Stand your ground, putting on the belt of truth and the body armor of God's righteousness. For shoes, put on the peace that comes from the Good News so that you will be fully prepared. In addition to all of these, hold up the shield of faith to stop the fiery arrows of the devil. Put on salvation as your helmet, and take the sword of the Spirit, which is the word of God (Eph 6:10-18).

I have hidden your word in my heart, that I might not sin against you (Ps 119:11).

He replied, 'What is impossible for people is possible with God' (Luke 18:27).

The Lord will fight for you. If you let him, he will stand with you. You can be victorious over temptation because he is there. When temptations knock on your door, you need to ask Jesus to open it.

CHAPTER FOUR
YOU CAN befriend the world's greatest evangelist

No, it is not Billy or Franklin Graham. It is not Andy Stanley or any TV-evangelist. You can find the world's greatest evangelist right in your own home.

The Bible has been printed more often than any other book in the world. The Bible Society of Britain calculates that between the years 1816 and 2007, the number of printed copies topped 7.5 billion. This does not include the digital editions that have been added the last few years. While the New Testament has been translated in approximately 1,400 languages, the entire Bible has been published in more than 450 languages. Furthermore, the Gospel of Mark has been translated in over 2,300 languages, representing over 90% of the world's population. Today there are some 1,900 languages representing 180 million people where translation work has not yet begun.

Since its inception, the United States has been a Bible-reading nation. That is clear by the Constitution and the Bill of Rights. Almost every state constitution invokes the name "Almighty God,' taken from the Bible. It was not long ago when the Bible was used to teach basic standards of private and public moral conduct. The Bible has been the foundation of the laws and judicial system for most of the Western world.

Taking note of the Bible is important

Many of the US presidents referred to the importance of the Bible. Here are a few of them:

> "It is impossible to rightly govern the world without God and the Bible."
> George Washington

> "The Bible is the book of all others, to be read at all ages and in all conditions of human life."
> John Quincy Adams

> "All things desirable to men are contained in the Bible."
> Abraham Lincoln

> "The Bible is the rock on which our republic rests."
> Andrew Jackson

> "We are indebted to the Book of Books for our national ideals and institutions. Their preservation rests in adhering to it principles."
> Herbert Hoover

> "The Bible is the moral code of civilization."
> Harry Truman

> "Within the covers of the Bible are the answers for all the problems men face."
> Ronald Reagan

When I encourage people to read the Bible, they often ask me, "But isn't the Bible hard to understand?" Today there are many modern language versions, help materials, and even audio and DVD versions that make the Bible easier to understand for all of us. Mark Twain once said, "It ain't those parts of the Bible that I can't understand that bother me, it is the parts that I do understand."

As we take note of what we understand in this book, we will find that this great evangelist leads us to Christ, who in turn can transform our lives.

Touched by the great evangelist

The history of the Church is full of anecdotal stories of people who have been touched by this great evangelist, the Word of God. Let me share some "old" as well as brand new stories from people I have befriended over the years, from different backgrounds and different continents.

I have come that you may have life

In 1976 I met a young Ethiopian man who was working as a Bible translator and later joined my staff to oversee our Bible translation work on that continent.

Steeped in the tradition of the Ethiopian Orthodox Church, Betta had learned to revere God. But the teaching he received included nothing about life after death, so, as a young man, he was very fearful. His father's death increased his fear and compelled him to go the extra mile to fulfill church rituals. He read 12 prayer books dedicated to different saints and daily devoted himself to the type of fasting which was usually reserved for priests and monks. In doing these tasks, he thought he would gain virtue.

"The closest I came to any spiritual experience was when I bowed reverently to kiss either the church door upon entry or the extended cross presented by the priest, and when I was sprinkled by or drank the holy water after Mass," he remembers. "The Word of God was never presented in a way that I could understand, because Mass was recited in the ancient church language, called Geez, the equivalent of Latin. Geez was understood only by the priests."

During his primary school days, Betta studied English because in secondary school, English was the language in which most subjects were taught. Still in his teens, he won a three-year scholarship to a training institute for teachers in another region of the country, thus easing some of the family's financial pressures. At the institute, he continued his religious fervor, but during his second year he was diagnosed with leukemia and nothing could be done to save his life. He left in despair and without hope of regaining his health.

At that desperate hour and in a weakened condition, he went to the school library. Here, for the first time in his life, he discovered a Bible written in his own language, and he began to read it with intense interest. As he did, hope grew within him. Simply having God's Word in his mother tongue was an encouragement even though, at this stage, his understanding of it was limited. But when he discovered John 10:10, where Jesus said, *The thief comes only to steal and kill and destroy. I have come that they may have life, and have it to the full.* The promise of life seemed to leap from the page.

"Scales fell from my eyes and God revealed a precious truth to me," Betta told me. "Until that moment, I thought Mohammed had come so people in some areas of the world would become Muslims, and Christ had come so others could become Christians. Now, for the first time, I associated Christ with life — *my life.* That revelation stimulated my child-like faith to believe that, if Christ comes to give life, I would not die of leukemia."

That was 1964. Betta is still alive and well today, serving the Lord with much joy, overseeing Ethiopian churches which are growing extremely fast in Kenya and Ethiopia. Following his understanding of the promise in John 10, Betta committed his life to Christ, and the Word of God became vital to everything he said and did. Joining a group of 15 Christian young people, he studied the Bible. Their desire was to become people of the Word who put into practice whatever they read from Scripture.

When they discovered that the early believing Christians were baptized, they wanted to do the same. But when they asked the orthodox bishop in their area to baptize them with water, he refused. He explained that in the orthodox tradition, newborn boys were baptized after 40 days and girls after 80 days. To baptize them again would contradict church tradition. Unconvinced by the bishop's argument, the young believers countered that since they had not believed when they were baptized as newborn babies, they needed to be baptized again.

Then they read in the Book of Acts about the Ethiopian eunuch who, when he believed, was baptized by Philip. They returned to the bishop and used this Scripture to prove that an Ethiopian, like them, was baptized when he believed. They asked again what would prevent them from doing the same, but the bishop adamantly held to his argument. Disappointed, but in obedience to the Word of God and regardless of the consequences, they found a small farm pond used to water animals. There they baptized each other in the name of the Father, Son and Holy Spirit.

God's revelation to Betta was part of a wider phenomenon happening throughout Ethiopia at the time. A nationwide awakening initiated tremendous evangelistic fervor. It became foundational in strengthening the Church when for 17 long years it was forced underground by Marxist oppression. Today the Church in Ethiopia continues to thrive and flourish.

Come to me and I will give you rest

Over the years, I have worked with many Indian translation teams as well as leaders. During a visit in 1984, I noticed a young energetic man, called P.L.N. Murthy, who worked on one of our translation projects in Hyderabad. He was born in a small town in India called Husnabad, which means "a place of beauty." Having given up hope of ever having a child, P.L.N. Murthy's mother conceived when she was 45 and his father 50. They were overwhelmed with the idea of having a male heir to continue the family traditions and legacy, as well as to perform the Hindu funeral rites at their deaths.

Following his primary school education, Murthy and his family left behind their ancestral home and moved to Hyderabad, the capital city of Andhra Pradesh. His father, the eldest of 16 brothers and sisters, and his mother, the eldest in her family, were looked upon as the highly respected elders of their clan. Their word was law, and they settled all the family disputes. No one dared defy their authority because they were the custodians of the ancestral properties and legacies.

"Following Brahmin traditions, my parents' marriage was arranged by their families when my father was 10 and my mother only 5," Murthy explained to me: "Prearranged marriages have been practiced among orthodox Hindu families since ancient times, because they believe such unions are made in heaven before the birth of every human being. The belief that one is destined to marry a specific person sooner or later encourages parents to arrange their children's marriages before they are exposed to worldly influences and responsibilities.

India is a country of paradoxes. Rich and poor exist and work side by side. People are highly superstitious. Most claim to be religious. Murthy became accustomed to the ritual of waking every morning at 4:30 to recite Hindu scriptures. Regardless of seasonal changes, the family was required to take a cold bath fully dressed and wear the wet clothes while meditating or memorizing scripture verses. Activities for the day did not begin until after this two-hour ritual.

Until the 1930s, when Mahatma Gandhi called for independence, India was controlled by Muslim and British rulers. Born in the post-independence era, Murthy saw India struggling to rebuild its economy and social life. He became very disillusioned by the social hypocrisy. After completing pre-university exams at 17, he returned home for the holidays. To pass time, he wanted to read something other than a textbook, so he began looking through books in the home library. There he found a New Testament. This was very strange because a Christian book is rarely found in an orthodox Hindu home. Christianity is associated with the low castes, and such caste distinctions were observed rigorously in Murthy's family. To this day, he has no idea where the New Testament came from, nor how it became part of his father's library.

Out of curiosity, he began reading. The first time, he understood nothing. Strange-sounding names, places, terms and events made the text boring and uninteresting. But he felt an innate yearning to read it again, this time more slowly. As he did, he began to understand a few passages. The teachings of Jesus were intriguing. When he began reading it for the third time, he carefully studied each verse.

As he read Matthew 11:28, *Come to me, all you who are weary and burdened, and I will give you rest.* Murthy's mind began to ponder the extent of its meaning in relation to the burden he carried from his Hindu childhood: striving to *attain* salvation. Instead, Jesus was encouraging him to come to him for rest.

"The religious exercises I practiced began scrolling through my mind. The meditations, and the rigorous discipline and rituals, were heavy and depressing," Murthy remembers. "My spiritual life was going nowhere. Finally, I said to myself, 'I no longer want to carry this burden that offers no hope, certainty or satisfaction. I will go to this Jesus who tells me he will give me rest.' Then without hesitation I said, 'Lord, here I am; give me that rest.' Immediately, I felt his touch as the mental heaviness lifted and tranquility filled my mind. The release was indescribable. I sensed peace and rest."

With this new experience of inner peace, Murthy continued reading and analyzing each verse to see how it applied to his life. When he read John 3, the phrase "born again" piqued his interest. Jesus was very emphatic about its importance, and Murthy knew it was what he wanted. He wanted to be a new creation. Hindus believe in rebirth, but this kind of rebirth was different.

By the time he had finished his third reading, he was a changed person. The words "repentance," and "cleansing" had shown him the path to victory. With each passing day, his reading offered new insights and experiences. It was a spiritual metamorphosis.

Under the influence of God's Word, he began abstaining from the daily Hindu meditation and rituals, and his father noticed. To see his son neglecting worship of the Hindu gods was offensive and, therefore, sinful. Murthy's abstinence made his father furious. As the only biological child of the family elders, he was expected to provide future leadership for the family's religious practices. Eventually, it became unbearable for Murthy's father to see his only son drifting away from Hinduism.

Pressure from relatives prompted him to deal with his son sternly. When the college holidays were over and Murthy was preparing to return to school, his father issued an ultimatum, "If you want to continue reading this Christian book, I will not send you to college. You must remain at home until you change." Murthy responded, "I am sorry, but I cannot stop." So he was kept at home. Believing his behavior was the result of inexperience and stubbornness, Murthy's father's anger steadily increased. Soon he could no longer bear the humiliation from relatives. Determined to change his son's mind, he stormed, "In spite of the warnings I have given you, I have lost face and am no longer respected. You have no place in my house. From now on, I will consider my son dead." In his anger he grabbed Murthy, opened the door and pushed him out of the house, saying, "When you are hungry, you will come back home. But don't come back as a Christian, only as a Hindu. We'll see how your Christ takes care of you!"

Murthy was stunned. He knew his father was unhappy about his Christian faith, but he never thought he would be driven from his home. He wondered, *what should I do? Where can I go?* He had never even met a Christian, nor attended a church. He knew no one who shared his newfound faith. But while his mind raced, his heart felt absolute peace and joy because he knew he had taken a stand for Christ and openly confessed him.

Murthy walked aimlessly for a long time, now knowing where to go. After a while, he saw a church and paused to wonder what went on inside. Entering the compound, he met a man supervising some people who were cleaning up the yard. Seeing the young stranger, the man said, "You are quite early for church. The worship will not start for another hour." Murthy replied, "I will wait."

As the service began, he realized that the man he had met was the pastor. After the service he invited Murthy to his study. When the pastor heard what had happened he offered Murthy a place to stay until his father would call him back.

When no word came, his stay at the church compound continued. Murthy studied, mediated and prayed. His needs for food, clothing and shelter were met in ways his father could not have foreseen. He had warned his son, "If you continue as a Christian, you will not inherit any of my properties. Everything will be given to your cousin and you will have to beg in the streets."

Murthy continued trusting God for everything. "In the early days of my Christian life, I made it a point not to ask anyone for money or help," he recalls. "I was determined to depend only on Jesus for every need, though at times that proved very difficult."

Murthy's father held out hope that he would return to Hinduism, but when Murthy married a Christian woman his hopes were dashed. True to his word, he left all his wealth to Murthy's relatives when he died.

After a few years, Murthy became involved in different organizations dealing with Scripture distribution. He had seen the power of the Word of God in his own life and now wanted to take this evangelist to others.

"It is my dream and prayer that, during my lifetime, the Word of God will be placed in the hands of every Indian. In this way, they will become aware of the Cross of Christ and have opportunity to receive the eternal life he offers. To fulfill this dream, we are taking Scripture to schools, prisons, hospitals, villages and all the places where people are located — even the remotest areas."

Brothers find the answer for life in the same book

A close friend of mine, Galo Vasquez, was born in Ecuador. Humble Catholics with strong moral values, the Vasquez family was actively involved in the church. From an early age, the Vasquez brothers served as altar boys. Eventually they would go their separate ways, only to meet again at the foot of the Cross. Galo shared this story with me:

"As Roman Catholics, we were very religious. On the Saturday before Easter, my brothers and I would walk through the streets of my city carrying a huge image of the Virgin Mary on our shoulders and ringing a big bell to wake people in time for morning mass. At one point, we were invited by the local archbishop to study in Spain for the priesthood, but my father rejected the idea.

From a young age, I had a consciousness of God, but over time I learned to acknowledge his presence and developed a reverence for him. Later, however, I noticed my behavior was no different from those who did not attend church. I may have been aware of his presence in church, but once outside its doors, I was no different from others. While church was a good place to be forgiven, it had little to do with my daily life.

After our family moved to Quito, I enrolled in grammar school and my older brother went to university where his life changed completely. He became an atheist, joined the Communist Party and, subsequently, became its general secretary. His name often appeared in the news and, when he returned home, he brought leftist literature with him. Sometimes he'd attend clandestine meetings with various tribal groups in the mountains, or he'd bring them into the city. Because of his political activities, my family lived in constant fear of the police.

When a military junta overthrew the government, my brother fled Quito for the mountain jungles because the new regime banned all political parties. One day, on a visit to a remote village for food, he met a British missionary from the Plymouth Brethren. They developed an unlikely friendship and after several meetings and discussions, the missionary led my brother, the communist revolutionary, to Christ. After daily Bible study and two years of discipleship by the missionary, my brother returned home carrying a Bible and was totally transformed.

The family was shocked. Catholics in Latin America did not own Bibles at the time and, to my parents, my brother becoming a Protestant was worse than being a Communist, especially as he couldn't stop talking about evangelical Christianity. Even though the family rejected his ideas, he continued to share his newfound faith. He invited us to church and encouraged us to read the Bible. One day I simply ran out of excuses for not going and joined him. The minister, a Canadian missionary, explained how the Creator was a personal God. This was news to me. As a Catholic, I believed in Jesus Christ as ruler of the Universe, but not as someone with whom I could have a personal relationship. Though the minister was not seminary-trained, he knew God's Word and could communicate it to young people. I was impressed. The following Sunday he spoke of Jesus *dying* for *my* sins. For the first time in my life, I heard about an alternative to penance.

After the service we went to the minister's home. Very inquisitive, I spent hours asking questions about Christianity. I appreciated that he never offered his opinions, but always used God's Word to explain things. Until now, the Bible had not been available to the common people of Ecuador, because we were told only trained clergy members could understand it. But as I began to read it, I understood and sensed a need to have my sins forgiven. The minister asked, 'Galo, are you prepared to recognize your sin against God? Are you ready to turn your life over to Him? Are you willing to invite Christ into your life as Savior and Lord?'

My response was typical of a Latin American Roman Catholic at the time: 'Sir, what do I have to do?' Years of penance, including crawling on my knees on a gravel road, flashed through my memory. When he replied, 'It's been done by Jesus,' it was both a revelation and relief. 'Your part is simply to accept what has already been accomplished and thank him.' My brother was living testimony of what this meant, so I was prepared, ready and willing to take this step of faith. We prayed, and I poured out my heart to Jesus, putting my trust in him.

I was 18 then, had just finished teacher's training and was working in a Catholic school. It was a government program to educate street children. I taught history, math, language and other subjects. Although employed by the government, I reported to the Jesuit priest. When I began asking him questions about the Bible, he became aware of my newfound faith.

'Are you having problems with money?' he asked. At that time, it was thought that if you were poor, it was advantageous to convert to evangelical Protestantism because you could receive food, clothing and, at times, money. 'We can take care of your money problems,' he continued, 'but you must stop studying this Book!'"

Through a miracle, Galo wound up studying abroad. When he returned to Ecuador, doors opened for him.

"God's Word changed the life and political revolutionary outlook of my brother," Galo said. "Seeing the miraculous change in his life led to my own encounter with Christ. The pattern continues to this day as we benefit from Scripture and pass it on to others."

Today, Galo Vasquez is the leader for the Billy Graham Evangelistic Association across Latin America.

A single Gospel tract leads to the conversion of many
Doddy Satyanarayan Murty was 20 years old when he moved to Kolkata from his native city of Vishakhapatnam, in the Indian state of Andhra Pradesh. One day, as he walked along the road near his new home, a young evangelist gave him a portion of Scripture which he was handing out to everyone who was willing to receive it. Murty went home and read the Scriptures carefully. He had never read anything like it, so after a week he looked for the evangelist, and when he located him, asked him, "Who is this Jesus that I am reading about in this pamphlet?"

The evangelist invited Murty to his home, where he told him more about Jesus. Gradually Murty understood more, as the evangelist met with him regularly. After three months, he asked Jesus to come into his life and his life was completely transformed. Soon thereafter, the evangelist baptized Murty and then returned to the area of India he had come from.

Murty received his own copy of the Bible and spent every day it. As he often sat outside to read, many people came by and asked him what he was reading. He took every opportunity to share about his newfound faith. People heard about this love that could give them a completely new life. He began to pray with people and they in turn became believers. Murthy had never been to church, nor did he understand what church was. Yet the new believers began to meet together regularly and shared and prayed. After a while, over 100 people had come to Christ. While Murty realized they needed to be baptized like he had been, he didn't know how to go about it.

Three years went by before the evangelist returned to the same area where Murty lived. To his surprise, he found more than a hundred new believers. Murty hugged him and cried out, "Don't leave me alone; help me to baptize these people!" After a massive baptism, a church in Kolkata sent a pastor every week to help the small congregation grow in their newfound faith.

The book returns to a country

In the year 862, two brothers, Cyril and Methodius, became missionaries to Moravia, today located in the most eastern part of the Czech Republic, to bring the Gospel to the Slavic people. In order to translate the Bible, they first needed to create an alphabet that included the specific features of the Slavic languages.

Initially the alphabet they constructed was called the *Glalolitic* alphabet. Its descendant script became known as *Cyrillic*. It is still used as the alphabet in countries like Russia, Ukraine, Belorussia, Bulgaria and others. The Bible took form and became the foundation for the Orthodox Churches in those countries.

During the Bolshevik Revolution and the following Communist regime, the Bible was a forbidden book. For years I helped supply Russian Scriptures to different groups that went to great lengths to bring the Bible into these countries behind the Iron Curtain.

For more than 70 years, the Bible was a forbidden book in the former Soviet Union. If you owned one, you could end up in jail. When the Iron Curtain fell in 1989, one of the most sought-after possessions was a Bible.

As soon as the wall fell down, the Bible trucks began to roll, especially from Sweden, where enormous presses printed literally hundreds of thousands of New Testaments. Shortly thereafter, Bibles and New Testaments could be printed within the country and made available to anyone.

I worked with two organizations that worked together on a project called *Book of Life*, a synopsis of the life of Christ from the four Gospels. Thousands of these were produced in Russian and introduced into the school system. Meeting with the vice-mayor of what was then Leningrad, he told me, "I am not a believer, but I have already seen the positive influence this book has on the children in the schools in my city. I want you to take these books to every school, and I will make sure that each school in every city of my nation will have this book."

Later I visited with the Ministry of Religious Affairs in Moscow who expressed the need for a copy of the New Testament for every person in the Moscow White House. It added up to 5,000 copies — one copy for everyone working there, from the president to the person cleaning the floors!

A few years later I received a letter from a Russian woman. She wrote, "I heard from my grandmother that there was a book called the Bible, but I never saw one in my life — until now! I got a copy, and I read it over and over again and I cannot see the end of what I will get out of it."

Touched by the evangelist leads to new churches

Raju was born into a Hindu background. His birthplace is located next to one of the two famous temples of the Indian state of Andhra Pradesh. Every Monday more than 50,000 pilgrims visit this temple. Naturally, Raju was drawn very deeply into religious activities. After reading all kinds of Hindu books, such as the Bhagavad Gita and Ramayana, he had many controversial questions, like "Why do gods marry?" "Why do they fight?" "Why are they sometimes like human beings and sometimes worse than them?" "Why do they hold weapons in their hands?"

He had no peace of mind, so he started searching for the real true God. He was thinking a lot about Jesus, as he had been told about Jesus by a man who was teaching street boys and girls to read.

As a young man, Raju was appointed to work in a government hospital. He worked in a clinic where the doctors, husband and wife, were both Christians, and they introduced him to the Bible. They shared from the Bible and taught him about Jesus. He accepted Christ in 1986.

In 1996, Raju started a church with 20 initial members. Today the church has increased to 150 members, as he has led more and more people to Christ.

Prakash is another young man living in the Angul district in the state of Odisha in India. One day he was out in the market buying vegetables when a stranger approached him and gave him a New Testament in his language. As he read the Gospels he became really curious about Jesus, so he looked for the man who had given him the book. When he found the man, named Mangaldan Harpal, Prakash was invited to visit his home.

Mangaldan explained the Gospel of Jesus Christ, and Prakash gave his heart to Jesus. He was encouraged to read the New Testament every day and pray to God. Later, Mangaldan asked Prakash if he wanted to open up his house for a weekly prayer meeting and he agreed. Prakash invited some of his friends to the prayer meeting, which turned into a house church. Now, there are 19 members in the congregation.

You need to get to know this evangelist

There is not a problem in the world that this Book cannot deal with. There is not a problem you face where the Bible cannot guide you on the path you should go.

Read it daily. Study the bigger themes by looking up words like "salvation," "forgiveness," "grace" and "faith" just to mention a few. Find and use a concordance, either in printed or electronic form. Read at least one chapter in the Gospels daily. Be amazed over who Jesus is. Take comfort in the Psalms and Proverbs. They will help you understand how to live. Here are some encouraging passages about this evangelist, the Bible:

And the words of the Lord are flawless, like silver purified in a crucible, like gold refined seven times (Psalm 12:6).

For the word of the Lord is right and true; he is faithful in all he does (Psalm 33:4).

I have hidden your word in my heart that I might not sin against you (Psalm 119:11).

I delight in your decrees; I will not neglect your word. Be good to your servant while I live, that I may obey your word (Psalm 119:16-17).

Your word is a lamp for my feet, a light on my path (Psalm 119:105).

Direct my footsteps according to your word; let no sin rule over me (Psalm 119:133).

Jesus said, Heaven and the earth shall pass away, but My words shall never pass away (Mark 13:31).

Get to know him through his Word. He will guide you. Open the book today. You can!

CHAPTER FIVE
YOU CAN use God's super jack

One day in 2013, I was on my way to visit a family who goes to our church. I wasn't sure which house was theirs, and when I finally found the address, I swung the car too hastily toward the curb. The impact sent a horrible shudder through the entire car. I locked the vehicle and went in for my appointment. When I returned to my car after an hour, the entire front wheel had collapsed. It was not a puncture; the entire side of the tire had a huge gash in it.

I knew that I needed to get the jack out of the car and figure out how to change the tire. My confession is that I had never changed a tire before. And worse than that, I didn't even know where the jack was located. I looked in every possible place, but no jack! Finally, I grabbed the handbook out of the glove compartment and began to read frantically. Where could it be?

In the end I found it, as well as the spare tire that was bolted under the second row of seats. Clumsily, I managed to release the spare tire, but I was not sure how to use the jack, as I had no prior experience. Fortunately, my son Paul came out to help me; he had mercy on his impractical father. When he arrived, he shook his head, and then began to show me how to use the jack. Now I know.

At times, we churchgoers seem to forget that prayer is indeed God's "super jack" to lift impossible situations out of the mire of hopelessness to the realm of possibilities. We talk a lot about praying for one another, but it is often more of an expression than something we actually intend to do. As a result of my involvement with *Serve Now*, I talk to a lot of people about giving donations to the ministry work. Very often, people respond to me, "Lars, I'll pray about it." Sadly, as I know from my many years of fund-raising experience, that often means, "No, I will not give."

Don Nordin, in his book *The Audacity of Prayer*, tells us: "Before reuniting with his brother Esau, Jacob prayed all night. He was determined to receive assurance from the Lord that his brother would not kill him the next day. So intense was that prayer meeting that Jacob emerged with a name change and a limp that would mark his every step for the rest of his life."

Have you ever had the audacity to go before the Lord with such passion for the burden you were carrying that you decided you would not leave until you were able to emerge with an answer? The desperate cry of the righteous in a prayer closet strikes a chord in the heart of God."

Sometimes we pray as if God is 8,000 light years away. The Book of James says, *You don't have what you want because you don't ask God for it. And even when you ask, you don't get it because your motives are all wrong — you want only what will give you pleasure* (James 4:2-3). Jesus said to his disciples, *Pray and you will receive. Ask and it will be given...* Did he lie? Or are his promises still valid?

When I was a young man, I read a lot of missionary biographies. I was enamored by George Mueller, who raised over 20,000 orphans in his home in London in the 19th century. He prayed every day for their needs: for food, for rent, for operating costs, etc. and God kept providing through people who were touched by God to answer Mr. Mueller's prayers.

One of his contemporaries was Hudson Taylor, the founder of China Inland Mission. Hudson Taylor did great work for God in China. In one of his books he tells the story of journeying to China for the first time.

"I have had all sorts of experiences in all sorts of circumstances, and when I have come to God and pleaded his own promises in his own Word, I have never been disappointed. I have been in circumstances of great difficulty and have been led to ask him for remarkable help.

I was nearly wrecked when I was going out to China the first time. Our vessel was becalmed (unable to move because of lack of wind), and gradually drifting upon the coast of New Guinea. We could see the savages on the shore. They had kindled a fire and were evidently expecting a good supper that night. When I was a medical student, some of the other students used to jeer at me because I was going among the heathen, and they would talk about "cold missionary." Well, it did look that night as if somebody was going to have a piece of hot missionary.

The captain said to me, 'We can't do anything else but to let down the long-boat.' They had tried to turn the head of the vessel around from the shore, but in vain. We had been becalmed for several weeks, with never a breeze, or any sign of one. In a few minutes we would be among the coral reefs. We would be at the mercy of those savages, and they didn't look as if they had much mercy.

'Well,' I said, 'there is one thing we haven't done yet. Let the Christians on board pray about it.' There were only three Christians on the ship. There was a black man on board, a steward, who was a very sweet Christian man, and the captain was a Christian, and I was the third. I proposed that we should retire to our cabins, and in the name of our Lord Jesus Christ ask our father, and his father, for a breeze immediately. They agreed.

I went to my cabin and told the Lord that I was just on my way to China, that he had sent me, and that I couldn't get there if I was shipwrecked and killed. Then I was going to ask him for a breeze, but I felt so confident about it that I couldn't ask him.

So I went up on deck. There was the second officer, the chief mate—a very godless man. I went up to him and said,

'If I were you I would let down the mainsail.'

'What do you want me to let down the mainsail for?'

'We have been praying for a breeze, and it is coming directly, and the sooner we are ready for it the better.'

With an oath, he said he would rather see a breeze than hear of one.

As he was speaking, I instinctively looked up and noticed that one of the sails was quivering with the coming breeze.

'Don't you see that the corners of the royals are already shaking? My dear fellow, there is a good breeze coming, and we had better be ready for it.' Of course the mate went to work, and soon the sailors were tramping over the deck. Before the sails were set the wind was down upon us. The captain came up to see what the matter was. He saw that our prayers had been answered; and we didn't forget to praise God ..."

Not only in the past ... but now

From having read no end of missionary biographies, I stepped into ministry and found that God's super jack was not only for people in Bible times or throughout movements in church history but that God also answers prayer in people's lives in the modern day.

During my early years of ministry, I was often in need of immediate miracles. I served a small country church where there was never enough money. I learned that if I put more money in the offering on Sunday, I could possibly be paid at least a portion of my salary on Tuesday! One week was especially difficult. There was no money and consequently no food. I had bought a can of sardines in tomato sauce, and every day I ate two of these tiny fish as my one meal for the day. By Sunday, I had run out. After the morning service, the hunger pangs were enormous. Finally, I went out in the courtyard and stood under one of the trees and prayed an intense prayer. I reminded God about the children of Israel getting manna in the desert, about Elijah being fed by ravens, and about the 5,000 people being fed as they listened to Jesus. Would the Lord listen to a young pastor who needed his dinner?

Suddenly, one of the older church members came cycling to the church in high speed. "Lars," she exclaimed, "we were sitting down at the dinner table, saying grace, when suddenly someone said 'we should have invited Lars.' So I ran out and jumped on my bicycle. Would you like some dinner?" Well, before I called on him, he had the answer already prepared.

On another weekend, we had some unusual bills and I was worried how I would make ends meet. The church was so small that I was both the pastor and the treasurer. That Sunday morning I prayed for a miracle, not knowing how anything miraculous could happen in our little service. Usually we were only 10-12 people meeting for the Sunday morning service and financially speaking I knew how little the congregation was capable of.

As we sang the second hymn, I watched through the window as a car drew up. A man stepped out and walked up the few steps to the church. Walking in, he sat down at the last row. I had never seen the man before. After my message, we sang a hymn for the offering, and as soon as it was collected, the man stood up, walked out and I noticed him get in the car and drive away. When we counted the offering after the service, there was a huge wad of notes, representing the income of the church for over a month! I never saw the man again. However, he was surely the answer to a very desperate prayer.

The Lord provides every need along the way

Recently, I traveled to India with a friend, Rev. Ben Foley from Allenwood, New Jersey. Together with a colleague, he had conducted some ministry in Burma and met me in Kolkata on the way home. Talking about prayer at the lunch table one day, he told me this remarkable story:

"Five years ago, I went to Burma and had some ministry there. After returning home to the US, I often prayed for the country and wondered if I would ever go back again. While praying in my church last year, God placed Burma on my heart so strongly that I wanted to email my friends in Burma and ask them to invite me. However, it did not feel right to do that, so I didn't. Then, my email account was hacked. I sent out my new email address to all my contacts, not even thinking that one of them was in Burma. A few days later, I received an invitation to come and minister. God had answered my prayer, and I said yes.

However, I realized that a few days in Burma was not enough. I prayed for a way to extend the trip but did not know how it would happen. Last September, you and I had lunch together, and suddenly I simply asked, 'Lars, you are not going to be in India first week of February are you?' and you answered, 'that is exactly the time I am planning to be there.' Another answered prayer.

I had invited the worship leader of the church to go with me, and as the departure date approached, I became really nervous. Neither of us had the funds needed for such a trip, and while we felt God's clear guidance to go, it did not feel right to ask the congregation. So we prayed. Knowing that God can meet every possible and impossible need, I tried to put my fear aside. One Sunday morning, one of our members placed a huge amount in the offering, specifically dedicated to our mission trip, covering both airfares and lodgings in both Burma and India. God had again answered my prayers."

When we were attending church in Naperville, Illinois, we watched a young man grow up in the youth group and eventually marry Lora, the pastor's daughter. Today, Mark Batterson pastors a church in Washington, D.C. and has become a much-read author and well-known speaker outside of his church.

In one of his books on prayer, Mark tells a story of one of those impossible prayers. They needed a huge sum of money to purchase a property. The church had no resources of that magnitude, but Mark kept on praying. One day, he received a phone call from some gentlemen he did not even know, and this is what they said, "We have observed you, and because you have vision beyond your resources we will give you three million dollars without any strings attached." God answers impossible prayers.

Too big for God?
There are times I have prayed, but with the deep-down sense that "this one is too big for God." How can I judge him like that? However, that is how we often reason. Lord, I believe you can heal a common cold and perhaps even trace away a fever. You did that with Peter's mother-in-law, after all. But my friend has terminal cancer. Can you answer my prayer — or is that too big for you?

During my 50 years in ministry, I have learned that the Lord always answers — in his way. If his purpose is to bring people home to him, he will do that. If there is a task for someone to do, he will reverse the sickness and make the person stay here on earth. He is an awesome God. All he asks us to do is to pray, and he will answer in his own way.

A few years ago a friend of ours went through a divorce. While the man talked to me about 30 minutes every day, it became obvious that there was not a single possibility that this marriage could ever be healed. He asked Doreen and me to pray, and we did, but it was hard to believe that God would step in. Months turned to a year and more. We prayed every day. The man stopped phoning, and we believed it was simply a lost cause. Then one day he called me with such joy in his voice, saying, "We have remarried. God did a miracle! Thank you for your prayers." What seemed humanly impossible, God turned into a wonderful answer to prayer.

Great Promises

There are some huge promises in Scripture about prayer. *I am going to the Father. You can ask for anything in my name, and I will do it, so that the Son can bring glory to the Father. Yes, ask me for anything in my name, and I will do it!* (John 14:13-14)

Just before he made this enormous promise, Jesus said, *I tell you the truth, anyone who believes in me will do the same works I have done, and even greater works, because I am going to be with the Father* (John 14:12).

That is so bold, that it is hard to fathom. Even greater things? It would be acceptable to just do half of it. I would be so satisfied if I could do even 10 percent of what Jesus did. However, most of us settle with none of it. We believe in him, but we are not doing what he did.

Unfortunately, many of us look at these words as personal promises for material benefits. Lord, give me the opportunity to write blank checks. I need two Mercedes Benz cars! But the context of Jesus' promises is that we should do it according to his will so he can bring glory to his father.

Today, you and I and the entire Church need to pray bold prayers to enable the Church to do what Jesus was doing — to proclaim the kingdom of God. He gave sight to the blind, he healed the sick, delivered the demon-possessed, all through the power of prayer. In the Book of Acts, the disciples did the same things as Jesus did, through the power of prayer.

Peter writes about earnest prayer. *The end of the world is coming soon. Therefore, be earnest and disciplined in your prayers* (1 Peter 4:7). That is prayer that does not give up, that keeps on believing, even when the odds do not look good. Luke expresses it like this: *If you keep knocking long enough, he will get up and give you whatever you need because of your shameless persistence* (Luke 11:8).

Is using God's super jack a priority for you?

Is prayer a priority? Are you praying, not just for answers to prayer, but according to how Jesus taught his disciples to pray?

I think they felt like we often do and simply exclaimed, *Lord, teach us to pray* (Luke 11:1). He did! He gave them a prayer that has been repeated every day on every continent for over 2,000 years. It is so profound and yet so simple.

Our Father in heaven, hallowed be your name, your kingdom come, your will be done on earth as it is in heaven. Give us today our daily bread. Forgive us our debts, as we also have forgiven our debtors. And lead us not into temptation, but deliver us from the evil one (Matt 6:9-13).

We call this the Lord's Prayer. It helps us as God's children to begin praying by adoring him. We focus our thoughts on the father's holiness and magnificence. We also find that we have a friend in our heavenly father.

We continue by submitting to his will, both here on earth and in heaven. Being submissive to God is the only way for our prayers to be answered. *This is the confidence we have in approaching God: that if we ask anything according to his will, he hears us* (1 John 5:14).

The prayer for our daily needs is probably the most common one. Whether we deal with a critical illness, financial distress, family issues or any other special circumstance, we need the assurance that God is able and willing to step into our daily lives and help us — either by relieving the source of our distress or by giving us his own strength, so we can survive the pain or temptation of the moment.

Some of us pray for our daily need while others pray for their daily greed. "Lord, give me, give me, and give me." The Lord is not like Santa Claus, waiting for our wish lists every day. *Dear friends, if our hearts do not condemn us, we have confidence before God and receive from him anything we ask, because we keep his commands and do what pleases him* (1 John 3:21-22).

Asking for forgiveness and forgiving others are probably the most reluctant prayers most of us pray. *And forgive us our sins, as we forgive our debtors.* I can easily ask to be forgiven, but it is harder to go to others and forgive them if they have hurt me. We all need to pray a prayer of repentance as we have all missed the mark and come short of the glory of God. When we receive God's acceptance through the cleansing blood of Jesus Christ, we recognize our personal need for forgiveness and repentance.

And lead us not into temptation, but deliver us from evil. Jesus faced temptation on several occasions. In every instance, he displayed a submissive attitude and acted in obedience to God. God never tempts us, nor does he isolate us from facing decisions. A prayer of deliverance not only requires a humble attitude, but demands action. And when we pray to be delivered, God does step in.

In a prayer of deliverance we are affirming that God truly is our deliverer from all forms of evil. *The Lord will rescue me from every evil attack and will bring me safely to his heavenly kingdom* (2 Tim 4:18).

He can, and therefore you can.

CHAPTER SIX
YOU CAN be guided by something better than a GPS

God has not left us poverty-stricken. He has promised to guide our every step. Just as a GPS helps us to get to our right destination, God's Spirit can guide us though our lives. And his guidance is far better. Do you want to hear his voice or do you want to drown it out?

Many years ago I lived in a small town on the east coast of Sweden, where I pastored a very tiny Salvation Army church. One day I was at the barber shop having a haircut when suddenly the barber turned to me and simply said, "A British registered ship docked at the harbor this morning." I gave it no further thought until I was reading my Bible that afternoon. That still voice of the Holy Spirit kept nudging me, "Go down to the harbor. A sailor needs you right now!" I thought the entire idea was silly, but I decided to take my moped down to the harbor. I was stopped by the guard at the harbor gate, and I simply said: "I have a message for a man on the British ship." Seeing my Salvation Army uniform, he let me through.

As I rode up to the side of the ship and towards the gangway, I saw several sailors hanging over the ship's side, smoking. When they saw me, they began to shout to each other, "He is here! He is here!"

As I walked on board, they explained to me that one of the sailors was sitting in his cabin crying, absolutely beside himself, and his mates did not know why. Several times he had sobbed,

"Send for the Salvation Army. Send for the Salvation Army." But his friends told him that would be pointless because no one spoke English in Sweden.

I entered the cabin, and a rough but heart-broken British sailor grabbed my hands and attempted to tell his sad story. He had wandered far from his mother's prayers and somehow the Holy Spirit had convicted him during this particular journey. We prayed together and, as far as I could see, he understood what we were doing. Fortunately, I had brought an English New Testament with me and gave it to him.

As it would be Sunday the following day, I drew him a map of the church's location and welcomed him to the Sunday morning service, not having much hope that he would turn up. Sunday came, I started the service, and no sailor was present. But then the door swung open, and there he was. That turned out to be one of the few times I interpreted myself as I preached. After taking him out to lunch, where I further explained the Gospel and the first steps of discipleship, I gave him some contact addresses to the Salvation Army in England. As I waved farewell to him, I marveled once again over the Holy Spirit's guidance and the clarity of his instructions.

God still speaks to us

God speaks to us through his Word, through others, and through our dreams as well as through our circumstances. He also speaks to us directly in a still small voice, right into our hearts. Learning to tune out all the distractions and distinguish between his voice, our own voice or the voice of the enemy is both possible and highly desirable.

The Lord orders our steps

The Bible tells us our steps are "ordered," It could be compared to ordering food in a restaurant. You order as much as you can eat. In the same way, God orders our steps in the amount and progression that we are able to take. *The steps of a good man are ordered by the Lord, and he delights in his way* (Ps 37:23).

The Bible further says, *A man's heart plans his way, But the Lord directs his steps* (Prov 16:9).

The Lord directs our paths

Trust in the Lord with all your heart, and lean not on your own understanding; in all your ways acknowledge him, and he shall direct your paths (Prov 3:5). We find out where he wants us to go by acknowledging him in all our ways.

We can learn to know God's directions through the following means:

Prayer

In order for God to speak to us, we need to be in his presence, actively listening for his voice. One way to sense God's leading in our lives is to spend time in prayer.

Look at the prayer of David, who was called "a man after God's own heart." David was a king, yet he took the time to pray to the Lord God Almighty, asking God to show him his ways and teach him his paths. *Show me your ways, O Lord; teach me your paths* (Ps 25:4). *Direct my steps by your Word* (Ps 119:136).

Take God at his word when you pray. Remember what he has promised: *I will instruct you and teach you in the way you should go; I will guide you with my eye* (Ps 32:8).

Tell him, "Lord Jesus, I am here to ask for your directions in my life. I do not want to go down my own path; instead, take me in your ways, Lord." You will soon see God coming through.

The Word of God

God speaks to us through his written word as we study and meditate upon it.

God's word is the lamp unto your feet and a light to your path (Ps 119:105). After you have prayed, do not expect a prophet to come out and put his hand on you to give you a prophecy. Instead, expect God to reveal things from his heart to yours. He wants you to know his ways from his word.

While you are going through the Word of God, listen to the Holy Spirit. Write down the impressions and ideas he gives you. Let the truth he reveals to you settle in and begin to work in you.

Listening to the voice of the Holy Spirit

The thing that we need to understand is that we cannot hurry God into anything. The Bible tells us to "wait upon the Lord." This is so important to our spiritual walk. When our heart is in the right place, we will hear him speak to us.

Isaiah 30:21 says, *Your ears shall hear a word behind you, saying, 'This is the way, walk in it. Whenever you turn to the right hand or whenever you turn to the left.'*

Jesus said in John 10:27, *My sheep hear my voice, and I know them, and they follow me.* We need to practice fine tuning our spiritual ears, so that we can hear him.

Circumstances

Many times, God will cause doors to open or others to close. If we are walking in obedience to him, we have to assume that events in our lives are ordered by God. They don't just happen by chance. When you see a door has opened up to you, it may be because God wants you to go through it!

Others

God can use other believers to show us his direction. Sometimes we will be singing a song in church, or we will be reading a Christian book, or hear a pastor's message, or one of our friends will say something that will show us God's will.

God can reveal his direction to us through any of these ways. But even when he does, it is still sometimes difficult to discern God's plan for our lives.

Jesus said in Matthew 18:16 *...by the word of two or three witnesses every word may be established.* This is a good principle to follow when you are trying to figure out God's plan. There have been times in my life when I simply had to take that first step of faith, and after I did, God confirmed his plan for me. You may sense God asking you to do this, but remember: God understands our human weaknesses. If we sincerely seek him and are willing to obey his word, he will usually affirm his will for us in several different ways.

Finally, rely on God's promise. *...and the sheep follow him because they know his voice. And a stranger they simply will not follow, but will flee from him, because they do not know the voice of strangers* (John 10:4-5).

God will guide you. You can follow his GPS.

CHAPTER SEVEN
YOU CAN receive gifts
every day of the year

I love birthdays. Someone once said, "It is good to have birthdays; it means you live longer." At my age, that is something to hope for every day. I can remember my birthdays back to the time I turned three years old. I had one big desire and that was to get a three-wheeler with a bell on the handle bar. My parents had sacrificed a lot to be able to buy me one second-hand, but missed my childish request for the bell! On the morning of my birthday, they woke me up by wheeling it into my bedroom as they were singing a Swedish Happy Birthday song.

To their amazement, I sat up in bed and began to cry. Between sobs I could only say one thing: "No bell, no bell, no bell!" I presume many other children have shown their dissatisfaction when their gifts were not exactly as they had imagined it. Since then, I have been very grateful for all the gifts I have received.

You and I can receive other gifts — spiritual gifts that are not linked to some physical birthday date. God has decided to bestow his children with gifts that will make them useful in his kingdom. Unfortunately, spiritual gifts have become the source of much controversy and confusion among believers. These gifts are meant to be gifts from God for the edification of the church. Even in the early Church there were misunderstandings about this subject that led to the splitting up, rather than building up, of the Church.

What are these gifts?

Let us get back to the source text, the Bible, and see what it says about the spiritual gifts that can be ours. They are mentioned in four separate passages. Here they are:

We have different gifts, according to the grace given to each of us. If your gift is prophesying, then prophesy in accordance with your faith; if it is serving, then serve; if it is teaching, then teach; if it is to encourage, then give encouragement; if it is giving, then give generously; if it is to lead, do it diligently; if it is to show mercy, do it cheerfully (Rom 12:6-8).

There are different kinds of gifts, but the same Spirit distributes them. There are different kinds of service, but the same Lord. There are different kinds of working, but in all of them and in everyone it is the same God at work.

Now to each one the manifestation of the Spirit is given for the common good. To one there is given through the Spirit a message of wisdom, to another a message of knowledge by means of the same Spirit, to another faith by the same Spirit, to another gifts of healing by that one Spirit, to another miraculous powers, to another prophecy, to another distinguishing between spirits, to another speaking in different kinds of tongues, and to still another the interpretation of tongues. All these are the work of one and the same Spirit, and he distributes them to each one, just as he determines. (1 Cor 12:4-11)

And God has placed in the church first of all apostles, second prophets, third teachers, then miracles, then gifts of healing, of helping, of guidance, and of different kinds of tongues. Are all apostles? Are all prophets? Are all teachers? Do all work miracles? Do all have gifts of healing? Do all speak in tongues? Do all interpret? Now eagerly desire the greater gifts (1 Cor 12:28-31).

But to each one of us grace has been given as Christ apportioned it. This is why it says: 'When he ascended on high, he took many captives and gave gifts to his people.' What does 'he ascended' mean except that he also descended to the lower, earthly regions?

He who descended is the very one who ascended higher than all the heavens, in order to fill the whole universe. So Christ himself gave the apostles, the prophets, the evangelists, the pastors and teachers, to equip his people for works of service, so that the body of Christ may be built up until we all reach unity in the faith and in the knowledge of the Son of God and become mature, attaining to the whole measure of the fullness of Christ (Eph 4:7-13).

Each of you should use whatever gift you have received to serve others, as faithful stewards of God's grace in its various forms (1 Pet 4:10).

Gifts for our common good

In 1 Corinthians 12, it is mentioned that spiritual gifts are given to God's people by the Holy Spirit for "the common good." Verse 11 says the gifts are given in just the way God decides — they are distributed based on his wisdom. Ephesians 4:12 tells us these gifts are given to prepare God's people for service and for building up the body of Christ. Although theologians differ on the actual number of spiritual gifts, God's Word clearly indicates a variety of gifts.

Spiritual gifts are special, God-given abilities meant to be used in service of God's kingdom — to benefit and build up the body of Christ as a whole. Here are the gifts, listed in alphabetical order.

Administration:

To steer the body of Christ, the Church, toward the accomplishment of God-given goals and directives by planning, organizing, and supervising others.

Apostle:

This was a title reserved for those disciples who walked together with Jesus during the three years he was here on earth. The gift may also represent people who will be sent forth to new frontiers with the Gospel, providing leadership over church bodies and maintaining authority over spiritual matters pertaining to the Church.

69

Celibacy:

To voluntarily remain single without regret and with the ability to maintain controlled sexual impulses in order to serve the Lord without distraction.

Discernment:

Also called "discernment of spirits." To clearly distinguish truth from error by judging whether the behavior or teaching is from God, Satan, or human error.

Evangelism:

To be a messenger of the Good News of the Gospel. He/she works for the Lord to bring people into the body of Christ where they can receive discipleship and teaching. He/she may evangelize through music, drama, preaching, and / or other creative ways.

Exhortation:

This basically means to come alongside another person with words of encouragement, comfort, consolation, and counsel in an effort to help them become all God wants them to be.

Faith:

To be persuaded of God's power and promises to accomplish his will and purpose and to display such a confidence in him and his Word that circumstances and obstacles do not shake that conviction. This is not the faith that is given to every believer, nor is it "saving faith." This is a special, supernatural faith, given by the Spirit, that God will do specific, great things.

Giving:

To freely share whatever material resources you have with cheerfulness, without any thought of being paid back.

Healing:

To be used as a means through which God makes people whole either physically, emotionally, mentally, or spiritually.

Helps:

To provide support or assistance to others in the body of Christ, so they in turn are freed up for ministry.

Hospitality:

To warmly welcome people, even strangers, into one's home or church and care for those in need with food or lodging.

Knowledge:

Also called "word of knowledge," it means to seek to learn as much about the Bible as possible by gathering and analyzing information. It may include a revelation by God to apply doctrinal truth.

Leadership:

To lead the people of God both conceptually and by example, with care and diligence, so that the direction of the church is influenced, and the people of God are motivated to get involved in the accomplishment of God's plans.

Martyrdom:

To give over one's life to suffer or to be put to death for the cause of Christ.

Mercy:

To be sensitive toward those who are suffering, whether physically, mentally, or emotionally, and to display genuine sympathy for their misery, speaking words of compassion as well as caring for them with deeds of love that help alleviate their distress.

Miracles:

To be enabled by God to perform mighty deeds of supernatural origin and means.

Missionary:

To have the ability to minister effectively within another culture, whether or not that culture is across national borders.

Pastor:

To be responsible for the spiritual protection, guidance, and feeding of a group of believers entrusted to one's care.

Prophecy:

To speak forth the message of God to his people. The message is usually one of edification, exhortation or consolation; although it can declare God's will in a particular circumstance, and in rare cases, predict future events.

Service:

To identify undone tasks in God's work, however menial, and use available resources to get the job done. People with this gift are the "hands" of the Church. They are concerned with meeting needs; they are highly motivated doers.

Teaching:

To instruct others in the Bible in a logical, systematic way so as to communicate pertinent information for true understanding and growth. The teacher and the pastor are often a shared office, but not always. The teacher lays the foundation and is concerned with detail and accuracy. He or she delights in research to validate truth.

Tongues:

To speak in a language not previously learned so unbelievers can hear God's message in their own language, or so that the Church body can be edified.

Interpretation of tongues:

To translate the message of someone who has spoken in tongues.

Voluntary poverty:

To purposely live an impoverished lifestyle so that material resources can be used to serve and aid others.

Wisdom:

Also called "word of wisdom." To apply knowledge to life in such a way that spiritual truths are made relevant and practical in proper decision-making and daily life situations.

Which ones are yours?

Jesus told a story about three servants who received resources to invest, each according to his ability. God is also distributing gifts to all of us, in whatever way it pleases his nature to give them to us. *Just as each of us has one body with many members, and these members do not all have the same function, so in Christ we who are many form one body, and each member belongs to all the others. We have different gifts, according to the grace given us* (Rom 12:4-6a).

So, look through the list. Ask God to equip you through the power of his Spirit. Then say thank you, and begin using the gift to further God's kingdom.

God has also given us talents

Talents are also gifts from God, but they are somewhat different from spiritual gifts. Both grow in effectiveness with use. Both are intended to be used on behalf of others, instead of for selfish purposes. A person, regardless of his belief in God or in Christ, is given a natural talent as a result of a combination of DNA. Some, for example, have a natural ability in music, art, or mathematics. The development of these talents may have a lot to do with your surroundings, as growing up in a musical family will aid a person in developing a talent for music. Sometimes God desires to endow certain individuals with certain talents, for his purposes. A biblical example is Bazeleel in the book of Exodus, who was equipped by the Lord with many talents to make artistic designs with gold, silver and bronze, as well as stone and wood, for the purpose of beautifying God's temple.

The difference between a talent and a spiritual gift can be identified as follows:

A talent is the result of genetics, environment or training, while a spiritual gift is the result of the power of the Holy Spirit. A talent can be possessed by anyone, Christian or non-Christian, while spiritual gifts are only possessed by Christians. While both talents and spiritual gifts should be used for God's glory and to minister to others, spiritual gifts are focused on these tasks, while talents can be used entirely for non-spiritual purposes.

***

So, seek spiritual gifts. Develop your talents. You can have gifts beyond your birthdays. Why is that? Because the Lord is giving you gifts through his Spirit and is developing talents within you as well. You can!

CHAPTER EIGHT
YOU CAN find the greatest love in the world

I love ice cream. I love the Broncos. I love ice hockey, especially the Swedish national team. I love to read. I love to write. I love to preach. I love my children and grandchildren. I love my wife. I love the Lord. Every person would like to be characterized as a great lover. But it is so hard to live up to.

Who can love perfectly? I am not very lovable most of the time. Who can love everybody, especially those that seem so nasty and unfriendly? Even those we live close to can at times build walls of ice around them. Finding healing and forgiveness, often seems impossible when those strong walls have been built up for years between your spouse and yourself, and even exist between you in your bed at night. Is any help to be found?

Yes, you and I can befriend the world's greatest lover, who has so much to teach us in this area. His name, you guessed it, is Jesus.

Jesus shows his perfect love

Jesus' love stems from his father's love. God's character is love. He loved us humans so much that he gave us the best he had, his son Jesus. *For God so loved the world so much that he gave his one and only son, so that everyone who believes in him will not perish but have eternal life* (John 3:16).

As Jesus walked on this earth, he practiced his father's love. He not only loved everybody he met — he also respected them. It is easy to respect the godly, the cultured and the intelligent. We think we are really spiritual when we manage to love other Christians. But Jesus loved all people. *You have heard that it was said, 'Love your neighbor and hate your enemy.' But I tell you, love your enemies and pray for those who persecute you* (Matt 5:43-44).

Jesus never despised anyone for being poor, like the widows he often met. Ignorance on the part of the Samaritan woman did not stop him from sharing the Good News with her. The prostitutes he encountered were not pushed away from him because of their immoral lifestyle, and the "untouchables" of his day, the lepers, received equal respect from the Master. In the eyes of Jesus, the entire world and all that it contained was not as valuable as one human soul.

Jesus loved people with compassion. Matthew describes it like this in his ninth chapter: *When he saw the crowds, he had compassion on them, because they were harassed and helpless, like sheep without a shepherd* (Matt 9:36).

Where would Jesus go if he came to your community?

If Jesus came to your city, where would he spend his first day? Would he visit your church and sit in the front row, or perhaps even in that special chair behind the podium? Probably not. He would more likely be at the hospital, visiting and praying with the sick. I can imagine him sitting next to a man who had drowned his sorrows in every imaginable drink the bartender could concoct. As the man pours out his pain to the stranger next to him, he would suddenly realize that Jesus actually cares. Most likely, Jesus would also visit the homeless and the prostitutes.

We may say, "I wouldn't do that!" Why not? Perhaps our churches would look different if, instead of inviting people to come to us, we went to them, and simply let the love we have learned from the Master rub off onto others.

Jesus was always with the sick, the needy, the hungry and the lonely. He cried at the tomb of his friend Lazarus, and he spent some time providing new hope for the bereaved, like the widow at Nain. When he touched the lepers, they understood that he cared.

Jesus was never irritated or critical of his friends

I am a Swede, and as a people group we are known for our punctuality. Jokingly, it is said that a Swede is born with a watch on his wrist. When you have an appointment or even when visiting a friend, you ensure you arrive right on the agreed time. If not, you always make sure to be early, sitting around the corner in your car, waiting for the appointed time. The Swede is usually not more than a few seconds early, and seldom a second late! I am known for this trait and have had to learn to give it up in several areas.

First of all, my wife operates on a completely different time schedule. She was 20 minutes late for our wedding. In the beginning of our marriage, I set all clocks 15 minutes ahead, but she soon caught up with my secret schemes. We are getting close to having been married for 50 years, but we still learn new ways to adjust to each other.

Secondly, I spend a lot of my work time in areas where time is not of great importance. While ministering in Nigeria, I learned that if the meeting was announced for four p.m. and I turned up exactly at that time, it would just be me and possibly a few chickens. Four meant that the meeting started at six. Asking how people knew, it seemed to be an unwritten code. If you wanted the meeting to start at five p.m., you would advertise "Four, prompt!" If you actually wanted a meeting to start at four p.m., you would advertise, "Four, Prompt! Prompt!"

In India, most conferences I attend really get going an hour after the announced starting time. No one seemed to be bothered by that (except me) so I have had to learn to go with the flow. Yet there are still times when I internally suffer from huge irritation and annoyance.

But the slowness of others never got on Jesus' nerves. He never made remarks or discussed the shortcomings of the disciples behind their backs. He could have exposed Judas, for he knew all the time that Judas would betray him. However, not one of the disciples knew beforehand.

Jesus was a great encourager. He publicly praised the faith of a Roman centurion. I wonder how Peter felt when Jesus told him he would pray for him.

The love of Jesus was so strong that he could correct others

A true friend dares to correct people he or she loves very much. If the friendship is solid, the recipient will be grateful. Jesus saw the need to correct Peter and actually told him: "Get behind me, Satan" when Peter suggested that Jesus should avoid the cross. When Peter and James used their mother to plead for higher positions of honor, he admonished them. When they wanted to take revenge on cities not open to the Gospel, he corrected them into a more loving attitude.

The love of Jesus stretched beyond what we could imagine

Have you ever hit the wall because of work overload? I have, several times, and it is a frustrating experience. You cannot handle one more phone call, one more conversation or one more demand on your time. Jesus only ministered publicly on earth for three and a half years, and during that time he was very busy. True, there were moments when he went away to the mountains to rest, and to pray. However, most of the time he was busy night and day. He did not have an assistant or a secretary. When the disciples tried to be his secretaries and told the children to go away, he rebuked them. People knew they could approach him and he gave his time to them.

The scholar Nicodemus knew he could come and see Jesus at night, because he would be available. People brought their sick relatives and friends to Jesus, most often after sunset, and Jesus laid hands on every one of them and healed them all.

The love of Jesus was a uniting force

Have you ever carefully read Jesus' prayer to his father in John 17:20-23? *My prayer is not for them alone. I pray also for those who will believe in me through their message, that all of them may be one, Father, just as you are in me and I in you. May they also be in us so that the world may believe that you have sent me. I have given them the glory that you gave me, that they may be on as we are one; I in them and you in me. May they be brought to complete unity to let the world know that you sent me and have loved them even as you have loved me.*

It is unfortunately true that when non-Christians look at us, they often do not see that kind of unity. When I visit a city or even a small community, I don't visually see that unity. Driving down Main Street you may come to the only traffic light in town. What do you usually see on each of the four corners? Four churches! These different buildings announce loud and clear, "We are divided."

It would not be so bad if all of the different churches on a particular intersection, or in their city block, used the same building. It would solve some of the mortgage problems churches have. Let me explain. By using the same facility, you just change the sign outside. At 8:00 a.m. you display the Episcopal Church sign. Their services are relatively short, so at 9:30 a.m. the Reformed Church puts up their sign. Their services are also fairly short, so at 11:00 a.m. the Baptist sign goes up. In the South you will need at least two hours for that. At 1:00 p.m. the Pentecostal Church can put up their sign. That one will be up for more than four hours. Then finally at 6:00 p.m. the sign states *The Salvation Army Church,* and their members come marching in with banners, tambourines and a brass band. We may not be the same church, but at least this would show a better way of using the building facilities. In this way, more of the money could be used to spread the Gospel.

Jesus' prayer is prominent in John's Gospel. It cannot be missed. It is there for us to notice — and to follow. He meant it to be taken seriously. It is translated into every language where there is a New Testament. It was one of the greatest and deepest desires of Jesus. It was on his mind as he prepared to go to the cross. We must follow its instructions.

Can you find a name of a church in the New Testament? It is referred to as the Church. It may have been the Church in Ephesus, Colossae, or Galatia. It did not meet in one building. It was spread out in hundreds of homes in every city. The name "church" literally means the "called out" of God. It is composed of all who have been called out of the kingdom of darkness into the kingdom of God.

I have only one sibling — a sister. My mother was born into a family with five brothers. She happened to be the last one born, so when she was born, the others were already there. She didn't choose them, and they didn't choose her. When she was born, it was a fact that they were her brothers.

These brothers were much older than my mother, and they were all very different. As a matter of fact, I was scared of at least four of them. The oldest one was 24 when my mother was born. He worked for the government, had been involved in selling 1,000 train engines to the tsar in Russia and had to go back there to rescue the order after the Bolshevik Revolution. He later became Consul General for the Dominican Republic. He was short, but had a personality that frightened me terribly. Another one of them was tall, a chain smoker, and had survived a cancer operation in his face which meant that one side of his face was severely deformed. His hoarse voice and brusque manners made it hard for me to be around him. The youngest brother was my best friend. He was musical, an entrepreneur and extremely personable. So, they were brothers, but very different. A short one, a tall one and a musical one.

It is just like that in the Church. You cannot pick your brothers and sisters. You can select your friend perhaps, but not your brothers and sisters. The Church is formed of all those who have Jesus Christ within them. Whether they are Reformed, Methodists, Baptists, Brethren or Pentecostal, if they have the son of God within them, they are in the family.

Who knows whom the Lord will make sharing a room at the same hotel in heaven? The Pentecostals and the Brethren together for eternity! Or perhaps Baptists and Presbyterians? Some Salvation Army soldiers and some Methodists? We had better get acquainted now. We had better accept each other now, regardless of our differences. As long as we have been redeemed by the Savior, we are heading in the same direction.

Jesus responded to abuse with love

Blessed are you when people shall hate you and when they shall separate you from them and shall reproach you and cast out your name as evil. Rejoice in that day (Luke 6:22-23a).

Jesus was abused by the people in his home town. He was abused by those who should have loved him the most — the religious leaders. In the end, Jesus was deserted by everyone. All those he had invested in and spent time with ran away and fled, leaving him alone with a governor and a king, who both abused him.

It is not what people say about you that matters most. It hurts, for sure, to be abused, but if you know who you are, you can get through those moments. Jesus knew what he was all about. Jesus never begged anyone to believe in him. He never wasted time on his critics. He kept his attention on his goal. He stayed focused.

Jesus did not strive to look good. He was good. He did not struggle to appear truthful because he was the truth. He had character. Make sure you never allow what others say about you to change your personal opinion of yourself. Jesus did not. He loved these people despite their abuse. That is the challenge that is before you and me today.

Jesus responded to betrayal with love

Have you ever been betrayed by someone you believed was your best friend? Perhaps you shared your innermost heavy burdens with a close friend, only to discover that the next day he went and revealed your secrets to others. You trusted your spouse one-hundred percent, only to find out that there had been an affair going on for a long time. Betrayal is terribly hard to endure, but it is still external. Bitterness is internal. Betrayal is something others do to you. Bitterness is something you do to yourself as a result of betrayal.

At the last supper, Jesus said: *One of you who eats with me shall betray me.* When Peter denied Jesus, Jesus did not become bitter. Jesus managed to turn that disappointment into a victory.

The love of Jesus was sacrificial

God so loved the world. It is because of his love that we surrender our lives to him. It is his love that reconciles us to him. It is not his might, but his love that draws us to him.

Today he commands you and me to love — this command goes beyond any other. He gave us this commandment: *Love the Lord and love your neighbor.*

So, who is my neighbor? The person living next to me? Yes. The people in my country? Yes. People outside my country? Yes, they are our neighbors too! It may even be people that do not love us. Remember the "Good" Samaritan? The people around him, in the place where he was traveling, did not see anything good in him. He did not think much of them, either. But when some of those people were robbed and beaten, he showed love beyond every possible measure.

The Scriptures tell us that *love will cast out fear.* Free from fear, I can be motivated to go to the unreached. The love of God must transform me first. God's love is irresistible. It penetrates the hearts of all who receive it.

We are created to be hungry and thirsty for love. A baby longs to be kissed and hugged. Throughout our growing up years, we long for love. As we enter the senior years of our lives, the need to feel included, and loved, grows even stronger.

This unconditional love that comes from God to his people is unheard of in some cultures. When we want to share the Gospel with our Muslim friends, we tend to look at rational arguments and massive theological apologetics. But one of the best ways to get a Muslim thinking about the difference between Allah and Christ, is simply to ask a very basic question: "Does Allah love you?" They are searching for this eternal love, but they know in their hearts they have not been loved by Allah. God's love is the power softens hearts to the Gospel.

Sameh Maurice, pastor of the largest Evangelical church in the Middle East, used to be my interpreter when I spoke at his church. In 2013, he was a speaker at the Evangelical Covenant Church's Midwinter Conference..

During his presentation, he told a few very moving stories. Three of his sisters and the husband of the eldest sister came from a staunch Muslim background. They all accepted Christ. This would normally be unheard of, and it created great difficulties in their family. When asked why they had done this, they responded: "This church has loved us as no one else has, even our own family." Unconditional love transformed them, made them open to the Gospel and then brought them to belief in Christ. They spent nine months in prison, after which most of them had to leave the country.

This church in Cairo has a ministry they call *Love Outreach.* They take gifts and toys and visit orphanages, schools and hospitals to express love to kids, even if those institutions are operated by staunch Muslim organizations.

To provide permission for the Christians to visit these Muslim institutions, representatives from these institutions have to fill out an application with the church. As of January 2013, the church had 120 organizations registered with them.

One day, a group of young people went to a remote center, loaded with gifts and a guitar. The man in charge opened the door and brusquely asked:

"Who are you?"

"We are a team from the church, coming with gifts for the children," they replied.

"Why?" said the man at the door. "Who said you could come?"

"Someone filled out an application."

"What is this?"

"A guitar."

"We don't allow music here. We are sponsored by Al Qaida. Now leave the gifts and don't come back."

The group stepped inside, began distributing the gifts, and hugged the children. One of the leaders at the center even started to cry.

"Sing only one song, please," she begged.

The team began to sing a song about love and about God's love. "God loves you, God loves you," they sang. Everybody began to cry.

"Please sing another one."

".... and another ..."

"Please come back, don't forget us!"

The power of love opens even the toughest doors.

Do we love them? Some of these people don't love us. The radicals tell us, "We have been ordered to hate you." Our answer needs to be, "We have been ordered to love you." Our Gospel is the Gospel of God's love.

Do we open our homes for them? Do we welcome them? There are thousands of "foreign" students at our universities. Eighty percent of them will never enter an American home during their years of study in the USA. What a fantastic opportunity for us to love them and care for them — even those who come from countries with another political or religious agenda. Jesus said, *Love your enemies* (Matt 5:44, 46). The author of the Book of Romans gives us the same message. *If your enemies are hungry, feed them. If they are thirsty, give them something to drink. In doing this, you will heap burning coals of shame on their heads* (Rom 12:20).

How do we continually reflect the love of Jesus?

The Church in Ephesus was a model church. When Paul wrote to them, he mentioned the word love more than twenty times.

Some thirty years later, Jesus spoke to the Church in Ephesus through the message of the Book of Revelation, and says, *"You have forsaken your first love."* How forgetful have I been, at times, to express my love for the Master? Somehow it feels as if I have trampled his love under my feet.

We need to learn to reflect the love of Jesus. This is his advice to us: *Whoever has my commands and obeys them, he is the one who loves me. He who loves me will be loved by my Father, and I too will love him and show myself to him* (John 14:21).

CHAPTER NINE
YOU CAN be humble

True humility is not thinking less of yourself; it is thinking of yourself less.

C. S. Lewis in *Mere Christianity*.

I have been driven many times upon my knees by the overwhelming conviction that I had nowhere else to go. My own wisdom and that of all about me seemed insufficient for that day.

Abraham Lincoln.

A true genius admits that he/she knows nothing.

Albert Einstein.

These are the few ways we can practice humility:
- To speak as little as possible of one's self.
- To mind one's own business.
- Not to want to manage other people's affairs.
- To avoid curiosity.
- To accept contradictions and correction cheerfully.
- To pass over the mistakes of others.
- To accept insults and injuries.
- To accept being slighted, forgotten and disliked.
- To be kind and gentle even under provocation.
- Never to stand on one's dignity.
- To choose always the hardest.

Mother Teresa
in *The Joy in Living: A Guide to Daily Living*.

True humility does not know that it is humble. If it did, it would be proud from the contemplation of so fine a virtue.

Martin Luther

As long as you are proud you cannot know God. A proud man is always looking down on things and people: and, of course, as long as you are looking down you cannot see something that is above you.

C.S. Lewis in *Mere Christianity*.

He didn't mind how he looked to other people, because the nursery magic had made him Real, and when you are Real shabbiness doesn't matter.

Margery Williams in *The Velveteen Rabbit*.

It is hard to be humble

A few years after we moved to the United States, one of my daughters took part in a country musical at her Junior High School, and I was asked to play the string bass in the little band accompanying the musical. One of the songs in particular has been stuck in my mind ever since.

It is written by country singer Mac Davis, and here are the lyrics:

> Oh, Lord, it's hard to be humble
> When you're perfect in every way
> I can't wait to look in the mirror
> 'Cause I get better lookin' each day
> To know me is to love me
> I must be a heck of a man
> Oh, Lord, it's hard to be humble
> But I'm doin' the best that I can

Humility does not come easy. It's like lecturing on Ten Steps to Humility and how I achieved it in four. Some of us are simply proud of the fact that we're so humble.

Jesus went as low as you can go

To learn real humility, we have to turn to the most humble man who walked on earth. This is how the Book of Philippians describes him: ... *have the same mindset as Christ Jesus: Who, being in very nature God, did not consider equality with God something to be used to his own advantage; rather, he made himself nothing by taking the very nature of a servant, being made in human likeness. And being found in appearance as a man, he humbled himself by becoming obedient to death — even death on a cross!* (Phil 2:5-8).

God's greatness is not just seen in the wonders of the universe, but in his humility — he gave all of himself and became like us. Do you realize that Jesus is the only person who had the opportunity to choose the family into which he would be born? He chose a young woman engaged to a poor, non-influential and unknown carpenter, living in a despised city — a couple so poor they could neither afford a bed nor a burnt offering lamb with which to dedicate their newborn son in the temple. Jesus was also the only person who was able to choose the circumstances of his birth. He could have chosen a palace, but instead he chose a cattle box in a stable. He chose to become lower than any of us, so he could be a servant to all. It is only when a person puts themselves underneath others that a person can lift others up.

This kind of humility is mentioned in Romans 12:2 when Paul says, *Do not conform to the pattern of this world, but be transformed by the renewing of your mind. Then you will be able to test and approve what God's will is — his good, pleasing and perfect will.* It starts in our thoughts. That is where we sow the seed of Christ-like humility; not by our actions and behavior in front of others. It is when we consider ourselves small in our own thoughts that we can genuinely regard others as more important. *Do nothing out of selfish ambition or vain conceit, but in humility consider others better than yourselves* (Phil 2:3).

Paul was a theologically trained man, and because he was a Roman citizen, had great standing with Jews and Romans alike.

Yet, to the Ephesians he said, *Although I am less than the least of all God's people, this grace was given me: to preach to the Gentiles the unsearchable riches of Christ* (Eph 3:8).

We are all rather title crazy

Have you noticed how eager we are to be recognized and honored in front of people? The Indian student, who is so eager to show others he tried, would not feel at all deflated by putting his name on his business card, followed by the line "B.A. Failed." At least he tried. It gets worse when we get to church. How many times have I heard the phrase, "How do you want us to introduce you? Reverend or Doctor?" My response is always, "Keep it to 15 seconds, and say 'Now speaks Brother Lars.'" Have you ever noticed how Jesus was introduced in the Gospels? Nobody ever said, "Now speaks Pastor Jesus" or even worse, "May I introduce to you the very honorable Right Reverend Doctor Jesus." No way! If he did not need it, why do we keep insisting on it?

He chose to be a carpenter which, in those days, was an unimpressive profession. When the crowds wanted to make him king, he slipped away. He told them he only wanted to be known as the "Son of Man." He did not mind being despised and rejected by the people around him. The only thing that mattered to him was his heavenly father's approval.

When he performed miracles, he was often quick to tell the people involved that no one should know about the healing. He saw the miracles as acts of compassion and not publicity stunts. Most of us probably would have sent out a newsletter, with flashy headlines and pictures of ourselves in the middle of the crowd, touching them all.

When Jesus raised the daughter of Jairus from her death, he told the people in her family not to tell anyone about it. Only after he had left earth was anything written about him.

One day he washed his disciples' feet. He didn't wait to see if anyone else would pick up the basin and wash the dirty feet first. He took the very first opportunity he could get to serve others.

Because Jesus had lowered himself before the Father, he could joyfully submit to anything that the Father asked of him. As Paul wrote to the Philippians; Jesus was *obedient to the point of death.*

There is only one time in the Gospels that Jesus tells his disciples to learn from him. In Matthew's gospel he declares, *learn from me, for I am gentle and humble in heart, and you will find rest for your souls* (Matt 11:29).

You can be humble if you learn of him. He could be, so you can.

CHAPTER TEN
YOU CAN be a survivor

Have you ever been very ill? Have you faced situations that seem impossible, wondering how you can survive one more day? Many of us have been there and have found that while the problems may not disappear, you can survive when you put your trust in the Lord who does the impossible.

That does not mean that the Lord functions like a vending machine; you put in the right amount of coins and your favorite healing, blessing or financial miracle will be the result. I am well aware that most people don't die while they are one hundred percent healthy. However, the Lord can and does always give us peace and strength to get through disaster, illness, financial crisis and even death, when we ask for his help. It is the change in our innermost being that matters most. You can be a survivor.

These are the days my friend, I hope they soon will end...

I have never been a healthy person. From about twelve years of age I suffered from violent migraines of such strength that I often could not function among people for at least two days out of every week. My wife used to say, "How can we plan anything for a weekend? Most likely Lars will be in bed, at least one of the days, without any chance of getting up for another 24 hours."

One day in the summer of 1993, I was sitting in my office and suddenly it was like a giant hand gripped the right side of my face and held it so tight I wanted to scream. My teeth clenched and my neck became stiff. My assistant encouraged me to go to a chiropractor, which I did. Before the chiropractor began any manipulations, he took my blood pressure and immediately said, "I'm going to drive you to the emergency room. Right now!" After several tests and a lot of various medications, the doctors sent me home without being sure what had happened.

Several days later, with no change, I decided I should see a neurologist. After a few minutes in his office, he looked at me and said, "You have had a spontaneous dissection of the carotid artery." At that point I fainted and fell to the floor.

After a short ambulance journey, I came around and found myself in the emergency room. One of the physicians described the procedures which were ahead of me. He handed me a form on a clipboard and told me, "You have to sign this release form. There is a possibility you may not survive this test." As I held the pen in my shaking hand, the words from the Book of Psalms came to me. *Teach us to number our days, that we may gain a heart of wisdom* (Ps 90:12).

At that point, I was 49 years old and had lived some 17,900 days. Suddenly my Day-Planner had no value. The appointments in the following week and the trip to Australia in a few weeks meant nothing any more. My only prayer was, "Lord, give me another day. And by the way, if you have a task for me to do, let me wake up every morning being thankful that you make me live another twenty-four hours."

They could not operate because the dissection was behind the bone in my head. So, after a lot of medication, including blood thinners, I slowly came back to health again. One of the physicians told me, "Don't do anything strenuous. It just takes one little bump, and your days are over!" I thanked him, left the hospital and within a week noticed that my migraines were gone! Many people's prayers were answered during that year. I found I could survive a bit longer.

About six years later, my wife noticed a spot on my cheek, "Check it out next time you go to your doctor," she encouraged me. I did, and he did not think it was anything to worry about. A year later it had grown and begun to bother some, so I asked for a biopsy.

I was in the middle of aboard meeting when the oncology specialist called me. "I have some bad news," he began. "There is cancer in your cheek, and we will have to take away a sixth of your face to try to get it all. You will most likely never be able to speak normally again." Here we were, discussing my preaching schedule for the summer with the board, while I was being told my speaking days were basically over. "How many of these operations have you done?" I asked the surgeon. "This is a rare cancer, so I have to admit you will be my first case," he responded. "Well sir, I have to tell you," I said. "I cannot let you practice on me!"

We had only started *Global Action* two years earlier. Why was this happening? God had opened so many doors, and suddenly it was like life had come to a screeching halt. My constant prayer was, "Lord, I am ready, take me home if you want to, but if you let me live, I will work for you every day of my life."

After a few days, I managed to get an appointment with the Mayo Clinic in Rochester, Minnesota. Doreen and I flew there for the operation. The afternoon before the surgery the doctor said, "We will most likely have to cut the nerves in your cheek, and as a result, you may drool a lot and not be able to speak normally."

I looked the surgeon in the eye and told him, "Sir, I believe some higher power will hold your hand and the knife tomorrow, and my trust is both in you and in the Lord. If you let him work with you, it will go well." The operation was held on Thursday morning and I would be released on Saturday morning. I continued, "On Saturday we are flying back to Colorado, and that night I will dedicate my grandson during our church service. Then, when the stitches are taken out next Wednesday, I will fly to Sweden and speak 50 times in 19 days." "That will most likely be impossible, Mr Dunberg," answered the surgeon.

They took out a good chunk of my face that morning, including a spider-like sarcoma cancer. "You came in time," the surgeon informed me, "because if we had waited some more months, it would have spread down your throat and into your lungs. But, we got it in time."

Saturday morning we flew home. As they had not bandaged my 45 stitches on my right cheek, I turned the left cheek to the congregation as I dedicated my grandson. When I arrived in Sweden the following week, speaking in all those meetings, the leader of the first church I visited looked at me, smiled and said, "Dunberg, your face looks like it has been in a plane crash!" I did not care! I could speak! I did not drool. I thanked God for giving me the strength to be a survivor.

Five years later, I noticed that I found it harder and harder to get out of a chair and that my muscles ached severely in my arms and legs. After a few months, the pain increased, like a constant toothache in all my muscles. We went to the University Hospital in Denver for a biopsy and a battery of tests. The results upset my entire world. I was diagnosed with poly-myositis, a muscle disease with no cure.

The specialist informed me that the only way to slow this disease down would be to take massive doses of steroids. I found I was allergic to the effects of steroids, so there was to be no relief. Then the specialist told me, "You may have two to three years before you will be confined to a wheelchair. Then, after another two years, you will most likely be confined to your bed, as muscle after muscle will give up their strength and functions." I was not yet 65! Would I end my ministry in bed? I decided to fight the disease in my own way; lots of prayer, lots of willpower and a determination not to move to the next step.

Then I thought, "Joni Eareckson Tada can travel the world and minister in a wheelchair. I can do the same." But then I contemplated that the next step would be even worse. I have never seen anyone travel around the world in a bed to minister. "Lord, if that is what you want me to do, I'll be the first one!" The daily ache is growing, tolerance to pain is increasing, and I am not as fast-paced on my feet as I used to be, but I am committed to survive as long as the Lord wants me to.

Now, I found myself thinking, my suffering had to be over, because on top of all this I have been using a sleeping machine, a BI-PAP for sleep-apnea, for the past 14 years. Dragging it around the world in an extra suitcase all these years has been quite an ordeal. While the machine is a blessing to me, as it helps me sleep, it is still something to deal with each day. But it still was not over…

In 2011, the physicians noticed some abnormality with my kidneys, and it was time for another biopsy. The result? My kidneys are like Swiss cheese and function only by the mercy of the Lord. More medication, healthy diets that made me lose 40 pounds, and some physical exercise have lowered the risk of the complications which the specialists initially feared.

I hope there's not much more around the corner, but I pray that whatever comes my way, I will be a survivor till the day he takes me home to the place where there is no sickness and no aging!

You can be guided by the Lord of the impossible

Over the last few years, I have befriended a couple in Texas. One day, as I was having breakfast in their home, I was told a very encouraging story of survival.

Three days after Christmas 2006, Kristen woke up at 5.00 a.m. in her home in southern Texas. It was the usual time her husband Steve went to the bathroom and showered, but this morning seemed different. While she heard the shower running, there were other sounds that she couldn't recognize. Steve seemed to be speaking loudly, but she could not make out the words. It sounded like he was fumbling around and dropping things. Kristen wondered, "What is going on? Is he mad at me? If so, why? We had a great Christmas!" The noises seemed to increase with every second. Finally, Kristen got out of bed and made her way to the bathroom. Steve was out of the shower and was trying to get dressed, but he did not seem to have any coordination. He was somehow caught in the clothing closet doors and could not free himself.

"Steve, what is wrong with you?" The question was answered by some weird-sounding noises. He could not speak! She knew something bad was happening.

Gently she led him to the bed where he could lie down while she dialed 911. While she waited, Kristen laid her body over his and prayed that God would intervene.

As the paramedics carried her husband out to the waiting ambulance, Kristen began to call friends to come and take care of her three children, ages six, seven and ten, who were still asleep. She called her mother-in-law who had just spent Christmas with them, and when she told her what had happened, Steve's mother said, "I knew something strange was going to happen because the Lord has kept telling me about restoration these last few days." There and then they both claimed restoration for Steve's condition.

After Kristen had been at the hospital for a while, the Indian neurologist called her into his office for a consultation and showed her the results of the scans he had taken of Steve's brain. He looked at her with sadness and asked, "What does your husband do for a living?" "He is the Chief Financial Officer of an oil company," Kristen responded. There was a deep sigh from the physician. "And, what do you do?" "I'm a housewife with three children at home." Another deep sigh from the physician.

"Let me tell you," the physician continued, "Steve is not going to be able to do that kind of work again." "Will he be able to speak?" Kristen asked. "Probably not," said the physician in a low voice.

He continued, "The reality is that he will not be able to compute numbers anymore, and he will not be able to talk normally again. He might be able to do small jobs after a lot of therapy, perhaps working at Starbucks or McDonald's, but his career as it has been, is over."

Kristen looked the physician straight in the eye and said as calmly as she could, "You don't know my husband, and you don't know my husband's God!"

As the nurse administered painkillers to Steve, she told Kristen, "Your husband is going to be in a lot of pain… go in and see him and keep encouraging him."

Kristen sat by Steve's bedside and held his hand. As she realized how severe the stroke had been she gently asked, "Who am I?" He could not say her name so she continued, "Am I your daughter?" He slowly shook his head. "Am I your sister? Am I your mother?" Again he slowly shook his head. Suddenly she said, "Am I your wife?" He nodded slowly. What a joy — he was still in there!

During this time, Kristen was encouraged over and over again by a passage of Scripture that described what people felt about Jesus. *Everyone was amazed and gave praise to God. They were filled with awe and said, 'We have seen remarkable things today'* (Luke 5:25-26).

Remarkably enough, Steve retained his penmanship. His handwriting was the same but words were out of order and they were badly misspelled.

The medical staff rolled a TV into Steve's room and tried to have him watch basketball games, one of his normal favorite pastimes. By his noises and grunts, they understood that he was following the game. He grunted in the right places — he was still in there!

One day he grabbed the Bible and by himself opened it to the passage where Zacharias, the priest, receives the message that his old, barren wife Elizabeth is going to have a baby. Steve made Kristen read that passage over and over again, telling the story how Zacharias hardly could believe God for such a miracle and expressed his doubt, so that the Lord made him mute. However, after the miracle happened, he could speak again. Steve knew that there was restoration coming for him as well.

It was a slow recovery. For two years, Steve was in speech therapy every day. Kristen went with him as often as possible, learning the routines so she could keep it up at home as well. Of course, any type of work was out of the question.

When Steve felt somewhat recovered, he began to volunteer at a not-for-profit organization called *Second Mile*. After being there as a volunteer for a while, someone asked him what he had been doing before he had a stroke, and he mentioned he had been working with numbers. The organization needed some help in the accounting department so they requested that he spend his volunteer time in the back room helping with the accounts.

One day, one of my old friends, who was then a board member of *Second Mile*, former state senator Mike Richards, walked into that back room and saw a tall man sitting there hunched over some numbers. When he asked Steve who he was and what he was doing, Steve responded with some mumbles, not able to find the words he needed. Mike felt so sad for that young man. Today Mike Richards can hardly believe the changes in Steve's life and career, and he is amazed by God's intervention.

Someone from one of the companies that Steve had been involved with prior to his stroke asked if he could do a short-term research project for them. While Steve never enjoyed the work, he was suddenly back in the game; he was back into his specialty field of oil and gas. Just working in that environment, he improved tremendously, and his speech improved dramatically. Another company offered him a CFO position and he was back in the swing of things.

In 2010, together with some colleagues, he founded a new company dedicated to building oil rigs in China for deep-sea oil exploration outside Norway. Suddenly Steve was spending his time traveling between the People's Republic of China, Norway, Luxembourg and Houston. Today, while at times you may notice a slight hesitation in his speech, he is a brilliant businessman who has proved to his unbelieving surroundings that you really can survive, with God's help.

While in the hospital, Steve had a vision for India, wanting to see the Lord use him in some way for the kingdom of God. Since 2010, Kristen and Steve have been involved in impacting children and adults alike in India. What was once a vision in the mind of a paralyzed man in a hospital bed is now a reality.

Right now, Steve and Kristen are praying about the future. How can they achieve their goal to go from success to significance? Steve is praying that God will give him and his wife many years, and that they will be able to use their talents and resources to invest in God's kingdom.

What seemed like an impossible dream only a few years ago God has turned into a reality for Steve and Kristen. You can overcome your situation. Even if it looks impossible, it is not impossible for God. You can!

CHAPTER ELEVEN
YOU CAN have as many children as you want

Around the world, some religions have grown rapidly as a result of families having many children. If every family has 8-10 children, and their faith is as much cultural as it is religious, that religion will grow with an explosive speed. That is not what I have in mind here. While "physical children" are a blessing, and sure, you can have as many as you want, I am referring here to spiritual children.

A few years ago, I assisted a church with their planning. Before we immersed ourselves in the work session, I asked some basic questions, to get us going.

"How many have come to faith in the last 12 months?" I asked.

"No one," they replied.

"That's sad... what about the last three years?"

"No one."

"Really? What about the last five years?"

"No one."

"Why not?"

"We have been so busy with our church programs."

It is remarkable how often church activities hinder us from taking part in the only major activity God gave the church to do: make disciples. We need to begin giving birth to spiritual children. God has no grandchildren. If Nicodemus, as a doctor of theology, had to be born again, so must everyone.

Talking about God to others can be quite embarrassing because for many of us it is a private matter. But if all of us think that way, the church will soon be full of only elderly people and will eventually die out. We need to have more spiritual children.

Jesus sets the perfect example for us

Jesus always went around and shared the good news. His final command to the disciples was to go and make more disciples. We can hardly claim to be his followers if we don't take any note of what he still wants us to do.

At times, when Christians think of leading people to Christ, we have a somewhat "conquering" mentality. We want to share Christ with others so we can get more people added to our church, as if it was some kind of club. We focus on numbers, and getting immediately plugged in. "I'm so glad you are here. Do you want to serve in the nursery or on the cleaning committee?" But we need to begin to think about the people around us in a spiritual light. We should see their spiritual needs and how Christ can meet those needs.

Some people are lonely. They have no one to talk to. They need to hear that the person who conquered death and loves us forever will come and be their best friend.

Some people are really struggling with the meaning of life, with questions such as "Why am I here?" or "Is there anything beyond living 70-80 years?" They need to know that the real purpose of every human being is to know God and to enjoy him forever.

Other people have very low self-esteem; others are high achievers. And whether they are positive or negative in their outlook on life, most people get depressed at times. But Jesus knows that everyone is valuable and unique in themselves, and he wants to have a personal relationship with each one of them.

Have you earned the right to speak to people? Can they see evidence of a changed life in you? There are really five evangelists who people can read. Matthew, Mark, Luke, John... and you. If people see that your life is lived for Christ in a selfless way, they will listen when you tell them your story about him.

Don't come across as perfect. Christians don't always know it all. It is when we are broken and transparent in our failures that people will see us as human, and that is the very thing that often prompts them to listen to us when we tell them about the One who carries us through.

Jesus is the perfect example for us when it comes to relationships with people. He let them know that he was one of them. He explained that the Father had sent him into the world to become flesh and dwell among us. God sent his son to the people. Today, that son, Jesus, is sending us into the world with his message. They will not hear it very well if we drop tracts from a plane, or just fleetingly knock on their doors with a gospel portion in our hands. Jesus talked to the people where he lived and where he traveled. You have to identify with the people around you before they will listen to you.

Jesus enjoyed people. He went to parties and visited weddings. He was often seen as the guest of honor at the dinner table. He went to where people were. Jesus was also intimate with people. He let them know that he could identify with their problems. He could read their thoughts. He cared for the sick. He was approachable. The children simply loved him.

Jesus had compassion for people, and that is one reason why they listened to him. Do you show compassion to your friends and neighbors? Do they see in you someone they can trust and believe in? Even when Jesus was on his way to heal the daughter of Jairus, he made his way through a crowd just so a woman who had tried every possible and impossible set of medicines with no success could touch the hem of his garment and be healed.

But Jesus' compassion did not come with a lot of fanfare. Rebecca Pippert, in her book *Out of the Saltshaker*, writes, "His care was consistent. Never flashy. Sometimes almost quiet. Even after his death, Jesus demonstrated the very same care. If I had resurrected, I would have rented the Coliseum and staged the Mormon

Tabernacle Choir to sing the 'Hallelujah Chorus.' But in one post-resurrection account we find Jesus making the disciples a little breakfast!"

Jesus could also be exasperating, because wherever he went he produced a crisis. He made sure that people were presented a choice. You were either for him or against him. Sometimes we are too nice. We need to encourage people to do something about him and his claims. We should encourage people to take his promises and claims seriously. Even today, he will say to people, through you, "Come, and follow me!"

Barriers

When you encourage people to examine the Christian faith, they tend to come up with excuses, creating mental barriers between themselves and the truth. .

"Don't all religions lead to the same God?"
"Where did Cain get his wife?"
"There are too many hypocrites in the church!"
"How can miracles be possible?"
"Why is there so much suffering in the world?
"Isn't the Bible full of mistakes?"

These are just some of the barriers, and we could write a separate book on how to deal with each one of them. While it is good for you to go through some of these questions and create your own answers to them, we are not asked to defend the faith to everyone we come in contact with. However, we have been asked to be his witnesses.

I love the simple way Paul handled sharing his faith when he was standing before King Agrippa in Acts 26. First he spent a few sentences telling what kind of person he had been before he met Christ, hating the Christians and wanting to kill them. Then he told the king how Jesus intercepted him on the road to Damascus.

About noon, Your Majesty, as I was on the road, a light from heaven brighter than the sun shone down on me and my companions. We all fell down, and I heard a voice saying to me in Aramaic, 'Saul, Saul, why are you persecuting me? It is useless for you to fight against my will.' 'Who are you, lord?' I asked. And the Lord replied, 'I am Jesus, the one you are persecuting. Now get to your feet! For I have appeared to you to appoint you as my servant and witness. You are to tell the world what you have seen and what I will show you in the future' (Acts 26:13-16).

Then he ends by telling King Agrippa how Jesus is now using him to proclaim the Gospel to the known world.

Do the same! Tell your own story of what your life was like before Christ, how you met him, and what he is doing in your life now. No one can question your story. If you have access to a New Testament or a Gospel, give it to the person you are talking to, and ask them to read that Gospel. Ask them to consider who they really think Jesus is. He will speak to them, sooner or later.

I serve as chairman for a certain mission organization, and recently, a lady came to work with us. Just before she joined our staff in India, I had the pleasure to meet her briefly. This is her story:

"My name is Jyothi Rani. I am from a Brahman background. My father is a Marathi Brahman and my mother is a Christian. My father was completely against Jesus and against allowing us to go to church. My mother wanted to send us to Sunday school, so she used to say that she is sending us to be educated and then I and my sister used to go to Sunday school. There I learnt about Jesus and accepted him as my Savior at the age of 12. One day, at a Sunday school retreat, we were given an opportunity to respond to either become a going, giving or praying missionary. I decided to become a going missionary, to spread the good news about Jesus Christ.

At the age of 19, I was married to a government employee. Though I married a Christian, he was a nominal believer. After five years of our marriage, he started worshipping idols. My sister-in-laws and I used to fast and pray for my husband's salvation and eventually God answered our prayers. After three years, he came to know about God's love, was baptized and started coming to church.

In 1992, I organized a Vacation Bible School (VBS) with 40 children. Within ten years, I came in contact with 580 children through conducting VBS programs. Among them, 80% of the children were non-believers. They accepted Jesus as their personal Savior during those events. Today I have three children that I have given physical birth to, but spiritually I have more than 10,000 children in Christ. God used me all across our state of Andhra Pradesh. Being a full time missionary to children I also have had the privilege to train Sunday school teachers and prepare them to hold their own VBS camps. The Lord has also opened the doors for me to spread the Good News about Jesus to lepers and prostitutes. I still continue to visit them and help them by providing for their basic needs.

My vision is to reach children all over India and give them the opportunity to open their hearts to Christ as their Savior in their young age, as God says in Proverbs 22:6: *Train up a child in the way he should go: and when he is old, he will not depart from it."*

I am so grateful for Jyothi, who against all the odds from her childhood, and through a difficult marriage situation, has been faithful to present Christ in a culture that is not particularly open to Christianity. But I am no Jyothi! I will probably never see that many people come to Christ. However, every day I ask the Lord to bring someone my way who has never heard the Gospel. Please pray that prayer as well. You or I may never present to Gospel to 10,000 people, but even if each Christian that shared the Gospel was successful in leading only one or two people to the Lord during their lifetime, the church would explode.

There is no limit! You can have as many children as you want!

CHAPTER TWELVE
YOU CAN be a mentor to others

If I were to ask you to name the three richest people in the world, or the three most recent winners of the Miss Universe contest, or the three latest Nobel Prize winners in Medicine, you might simply scratch your head. Then, if I continued by asking you to name the top three movie stars in the world, followed by the last three Europeans to win gold medals in the Winter Olympics, you would probably totally give up!

We simply don't remember yesterday's headlines, or even the greatest people in the world within their specific fields. When the cheers have died down and their sought-after trophies have received a few dents or lost their luster, those successes are completely forgotten.

Now think for a minute and see if you can tell me the names of your three favorite teachers. Name three friends who helped you during a difficult time in your life. Name three people who have inspired you or have taught you something of great value. Well, that was easy!

You can have that kind of impact in someone's life. Years from now, they will look back and remember your name clearly, because you guided them through some real life-changing experiences, and you taught them to be follower of Christ.

While this chapter will teach you some basic mentoring principles, its main purpose is to be used as a tool that will encourage you to take an action by investing your life into the lives of others. As you have been challenged to be a Christ-follower, this is your opportunity to mentor others, so that they in turn can find courage to step out of their comfort zone and follow him. They will get a chance to experience what happens when we let God take who we are, what we can do and what we have, and make it into something effective for his kingdom and for his glory.

What is mentoring all about?

What is a mentor? The actual word is not a biblical term, but comes from Greek mythology. *Mentor* was the name of the wise and faithful advisor to Odysseus. When Odysseus went on long trips, Mentor stayed behind and taught Odysseus' son, Telemachus.

The actual Greek word means *long-lasting* and defines the relationship between a young person and an adult. Today, mentoring means a regular contact between two persons, where one offers help and guidance to another person. The person receiving mentoring may be going through a difficult period, meeting new challenges, working on correcting a problem or they may simply be in need of guidance along life's path.

While the word *mentor* may not be biblical, mentoring itself definitely is. Jesus had twelve disciples who he trained to become like him. He spent quality time with three of them as part of his inner circle. The apostles and disciples emulated his example. Paul mentored Timothy, Silas and Epaphroditus. Barnabas guided Mark.

Basic facts about mentoring

There is no doubt that mentoring is needed in today's society. We cannot do everything on our own. Young and old alike tell stories about people who have enriched their lives by providing mentorship in many areas, including spiritual growth, social interactions, academic studies, career paths, leadership and emotional issues.

Mentoring is needed because we are designed to need positive role models. No one can live or lead in isolation. We often need to bounce our plans, or problems off of someone in whom we have confidence. We need to ease the burdens of our hearts by sharing them with someone we trust.

Mentoring helps people develop the gifts they need to succeed in their tasks. It helps develop the individuals so they can reach their goals. Mentoring nurtures the development of spiritual insight, which helps a person learn and apply what she/he studies.

Mentors in my life

When I look back to my teens and the early, formative years of my ministry experiences, I think of those that helped shape my life and I wonder where I would have been without them. Hebrews 13:7 says: *Remember your leaders who taught you the word of God. Think of all the good that has come from their lives, and follow the example of their faith.* There are five people who I consider to be my close mentors. None of them are alive today, but their influence still speaks to me.

The first one was Berthil Paulsson, who was the same age as my dad. In his most energetic ministry days, he was often called *Sweden's Billy Graham*, a title that suited him perfectly. Berthil was an evangelist with the Covenant Church of Sweden, and during the 50's he was the key evangelist in the interdenominational crusade team called the *All Christian Evangelistic Team*. It was during their three-month-long Stockholm crusade in the spring of 1957 that I came to Christ and asked him to transform my life. During those three months of crusade rallies, I heard a lot of sermons. I don't remember any of them, except portions of the one Berthil preached the night I was saved. But I vividly remember the way he preached, the tone of his voice, the gestures and the conviction that rubbed off on my twelve-year-old soul. More than 55 years later, I can still envision him and hear his voice!

After I went into the ministry, Berthil and I struck up a friendship, often writing or calling each other. When he talked with you, he made you feel as if you were the only person who existed to him. His superlatives exploded as you told him about your successes and failures and challenges. He always had a word of advice. There was no ministry problem too small for him to deal with. He regularly called me on the phone. He was my advisor when we decided to move to Sweden. This was a real challenge for us, as Doreen did not speak Swedish and had never lived in another culture. His calming way of dealing with my fear helped us through some difficult moments.

One year after we were married, Doreen and I visited Sweden with one of the Youth for Christ youth teams from Britain, and when the team returned, we stayed behind for a week. We met with Berthil and his wife in their home. Animatedly he looked at me over a cup of coffee. "I am conducting a huge interdenominational *New Life* crusade in the city of Nässjö. Are you going back to England via Gothenburg?" When I mentioned that we were, he interrupted me and said, "Great! I want you to come Thursday night and preach for me in the crusade."

Traveling halfway down the country towards Gothenburg, I left Doreen, our daughter Carin, and Doreen's parents with a mutual friend, and drove to the city of Nässjö. The whole city knew about the *New Life* crusade. The choir was huge, and the soloist was one of the most popular gospel singers in Sweden at the time. I thought Berthil would be away that night and inwardly hoped he would be, but lo and behold, there he was sitting on the platform. The huge tent was absolutely jam-packed with people, some standing outside as well. That night he acted as if I was Billy Graham, visiting him!

Sitting on the platform, I panicked. What could I preach? Here was my hero, with at least another 30 pastors on the podium. My mind froze. Bible texts and sermon outlines whirled through my head and my palms went completely wet as the choir sang. One very obscure text came to my mind, with a forceful outline, but that was not at all what I had prepared. "Lord, help me!" I whispered "confirm this to me!" As the song ended and it was absolutely silent, one of the Pentecostals broke out in a message of tongues (rather unusual for joint services like this) and that was followed immediately by someone else interpreting. The message given was nothing but my outline! As I was introduced, I rushed up to the pulpit and preached my heart out. Literally hundreds filled the prayer tent after the message, seeking God! I knew beyond a shadow of a doubt that this was what God wanted me to do for the foreseeable future. Berthil's encouragement on that night has often been a reminder to me during darker moments of my ministry.

Berthil Paulsson taught me a lesson which I have tried to implement: every person, however young or inexperienced, is important and needs to be treated with respect, encouragement and interest.

George Perry was the Training Principal at the bible college in Sweden where I attended in 1962-1963. Perry had spent most of his active ministry life in the USA, pastoring in places like Chicago, Duluth and Minneapolis. For seven years he pastored an exploding Salvation Army Church in Rockford, Illinois. During those years, revival broke out and lasted for the entire time he was there, creating conversion stories that are still imprinted in my heart and mind.

George Perry had a heart for evangelism, for the lost and for seeing the fire of the Holy Spirit burning within his students. He modeled a Christian life for me in such a way that I knew that high ideals could become reality and be lived out.

George Perry had been involved in many revivals in the USA. Often, he would invite me to his home for coffee and just sit and talk about the times God's Spirit showed up in such a tangible way that people cried out over their sins, pleaded for repentance and were literally transformed as people prayed for them. He walked me through his huge library of books in English from various Christian authors, and as he took out volume after volume and explained its significance, my love for books just kept growing.

After I left the Salvation Army, he continued to write me notes and stay in touch. His death in 1969 came far too soon, but his life is still reflected in some of my behavior. George Perry left this mark on my life: ideals can become reality by living out Christ's values in everyday life.

After a year in Sweden under Perry's leadership, I was transferred to London and to William Booth Memorial Training College, where Clarence Wiseman was the Principal. He was originally from Canada, had served the Lord in Africa, and later went on to be the world leader, the general, of the Salvation Army.

He was a man who taught his students to merge academic studies with fervent evangelism. Often we would finish a "finals" exam one afternoon, and then immediately march single file down the street to the bus station. As we marched, I played my accordion. The bus would take us to some evangelistic effort. Sometimes we would wind up at a youth hostel, or youth prison. Other times we would find ourselves trying to share the Gospel with people who were going in and out of night clubs.

Commissioner Wiseman taught me how to deal with difficult issues in front of a group of students and staff. When, at times, there were severe breaches in personal relationships among students, his candor in dealing with such problems showed me a tender way to deal with complex issues without giving up firm principles. He also taught us that current events can be interpreted from Scripture. His passionate messages in front of the student body were often delivered with *Time* magazine in one of his hands and the Bible in the other. From Clarence Wiseman I learned that if the Gospel is shared in faith, people respond — even in the most unlikely environments.

Denis Clark was a businessman from South Africa who received a calling to preach in his thirties. Through the work of Youth for Christ, he moved to Europe and later worked as an independent evangelist across the world. I first met Denis in Sweden where he was holding several crusades. A lot of his preaching was focused on the deeper spiritual life of the believer. No one has ever opened up the Word of God for me the way Denis did. He modeled a prayer life and a heart knowledge of the Scriptures that did not just focus on the mind, but was filled with the presence of the Holy Spirit. He taught me to apply the Word of God to daily situations.

After Doreen and I got married, I worked for Youth for Christ in Britain, and I invited Denis to serve on the Youth for Christ board in Britain. Many were the times that he took on a strategic personal mentoring role in my life, dealing with all kinds of issues: from how to get more faith for our meager finances to questions of accountability and integrity. Denis was a man who walked with God, and God took him home in the prime of his life. Denis Clark taught me that power to live for Christ comes through a combination of his living Word, prayer, and the indwelling and presence of the Holy Spirit.

While these four mentors were dealing mostly with spiritual and philosophical issues, Harold Shaw, originally from Canada, almost 30 years my senior, taught me on many practical issues, especially about publishing. Harold had served with Moody Bible Institute, then at Tyndale House Publishers, while also operating his own publishing firm, Harold Shaw Publishers. Basically, everything I know about publishing, accounting, cash flow management, warehousing, turning over inventory, pricing and marketing, I learned from Harold.

He would often come to Sweden and spend three to four days with me, working 18-hour days. I was like a sponge, soaking up everything he could teach me. But in all his business dealings, it was Harold's spiritual insight that impressed me most. Harold had his roots in the Plymouth Brethren, but was also open to a deeper walk in the Spirit, uniting the love for the Word with the presence of the Holy Spirit.

Soon we became the best of friends. We traveled the world together several times when I became the president of Living Bibles International and he was a board member. When we moved to the USA, Harold became the "listening post" in my life. Almost every week I was in his office for an hour, and as I poured out my heart, Harold listened intently. Then he would always say, "Lars, I see three things here..." and the solutions would be presented for me to make a choice!

Far too early, Harold was hit by cancer. I served on the board of Harold Shaw Publishers, helping his wife Luci through some of those difficult days, as she ran the business while her husband lay sick in bed. The day before Harold went to be with the Lord, I sat at his bed, thanking the Lord and Harold for the tremendous influence he had been in my life.

Harold Shaw taught me that spiritual discernment needs to go hand-in-hand with the way we operate things. Listening and encouraging others to find the answers is often more important than telling them what to do.

Through the lives of these men I learned the importance of mentoring others. We may never know what influence we have. Our lives reflect into the lives of others. Who we are speaks much louder than our words. Our actions, deliberate or subconscious, are instruments of learning for future generations of people whom the Lord leads us to interact with on a regular basis. What an awesome responsibility we carry!

Paul was a great mentor. Jesus was the master mentor with twelve people in the inner circle and some 70 in the extended circle. He had time for them, and they knew that they could always come to him. Mentors can play an enormous role in any person's life.

Do we need mentors?

In their book *As Iron Sharpens Iron*, Howard and Bill Hendricks speak of mentors as "seasoned guides" and use an illustration from Bob Biehl of Masterplanning Group International to make their point.

"Mentoring is like a group of men scaling a mountain. If a guy is linked to another guy above him and that man in turn is linked to other men farther up the cliff, then together they have safety, stability, and strength. If a man slips and begins to fall, fifteen or twenty climbers absorb the impact and pull the man back from disaster. But imagine a man climbing alone, with no support system. He may achieve great heights. But one wrong move and he can fall thousands of feet to his death, without anyone hearing his cry."

Two are better than one, because they have a good return for their work: If one falls down, his friend can help him up. A cord of three strands is not quickly broken (Eccl 4:9-10, 12).

Mentoring helps us develop spiritually

Mentoring was the primary method of handing down wisdom and skills from one generation to another in biblical times. In a similar way, spiritual mentoring helps people come to know the Lord and grow into mature Christians.

Mentoring helps us develop in our work

Mentoring is helpful when someone wants to learn about a new or different area of work in an organization, or if they want to enrich their experience in their present job. Succession planning for senior leader positions in a church or an organization can be accelerated when it includes mentoring.

Mentoring helps in leadership development

Leaders need to be competent in many areas. A highly potential person considered for a leadership position, a person promoted to higher levels of responsibility, or a leader within his/her existing position, can learn from others who have high level competence in personal, team, and organizational levels of leadership.

Mentoring helps during a time of change or transition

Mentoring can prove valuable during times of organizational change, particularly when new business structures, practices, or technologies are introduced to an organization or church. Small group mentoring by an expert during the change can assist staff in making a speedier transition to new ways of operating the church or the organization. Because organizational change is usually connected with personal changes in the lives of staff, mentors can assist mentoring partners in facilitating a successful transition process.

Benefits to the mentoring partner

Most mentoring partners find that their mentors' investments into their futures help them gain knowledge, skills, experiences, relationships, and opportunities at a faster rate than they would without a mentor. Constructive feedback helps them steer in the right direction and bridge gaps in their performance.

The mentoring partner increases his/her self-awareness, confidence, and skill. He/she learns how to be disciplined and focused in planning the future. As opportunities to serve in a church, Christian organization or secular field arise, he/she can be much better prepared.

A mentor helps a mentoring partner gain appreciation of who God has uniquely designed them to be, so they can see clearly their important role in the kingdom of God.

Benefits to the mentor

People who have served as mentors understand that they not only give, but also receive blessings from their mentoring partners. As mentors teach, they also gain valuable insight, adding to their own expertise. Through mentoring, they experience continuous self-renewal, spiritually as well as mentally. They continue learning and staying connected with the world outside themselves or their day-to-day functions in a church or a Christian organization. Some mention the infusion of fresh creativity into their work as a natural outcome of examining options with their mentoring partners.

Mentors experience an increase in job satisfaction and renewed motivation. They frequently develop a close relationship with their mentoring partner, who in some cases even completes projects on their behalf. Mentors receive public recognition for their work; enjoy a sense of being needed, and get the opportunity to influence the career development of a talented young colleague.

Mentors often speak of themselves as the partner receiving the blessings. They receive an opportunity to extend their learning and life experience through the lives of their mentoring partners, but do not want to duplicate themselves in the process. Good mentors sense the importance of serving as positive role models and setting personal examples for their mentoring partners, so that the relationship strengthens the character of both.

You can become a mentor

Decide how many persons you can mentor at one time. I recommend three as a good number. Of course it can be more, and it can be less. Before you even start, check if there is potential in the person you want to mentor. Is he/she teachable? Is the person willing to give the time it takes? Is the person willing to set up goals for his/her life? Is the person looking for greater challenges in life? Can he/she in turn mentor others?

Get to know the person you are mentoring. Learn all you can about them. Identify their gifts and strengths and then build on them. Acknowledge their fears and weaknesses. Look for patterns that occur.

Expect excellence from the people you are mentoring. Set high expectations. Don't let them be tardy with appointments or assigned tasks. We live in the end times and this is the time God has given us to act. Time is simply too short to be nice! Model the same excellence for them. You also need to demonstrate confidence in their ability to meet your and their own expectations — just remember never to endorse perfection as the ultimate goal!

Affirm each person you mentor as a person of great value. Instill confidence in them so they can overcome self-doubt. At all times, attempt to endorse their dreams, while you at the same time shed light on unrealistic aspirations.

Share knowledge and experience strategically. Do not lecture, patronize or hand out lines like: "When I was a boy, I had to walk to school through the snow while my shoes leaked!"

Share experiences: "That's been my experience when similar things happened to me!" Share observations: "I have noticed that you seem irritated when you talk to so and so." Provide suggestions and advice: "If I were in your position I would…" "Here is something you might consider." "Whatever you think is working best, you should do ..." You do not give orders to the people you mentor; you are there to give them suggestions. Encourage and support the people you mentor at every level. Even the most talented person benefits from encouragement, and it builds further energy.

Always tell your story first. If you ask questions first, your mentoring time becomes more of an interrogation than a time of building trust. Use your personal experiences as a means to teaching, reassuring and connecting. Model humility, and show how you coped through difficulties, not how you excelled in everything.

When you do begin with questioning people you mentor, ask broad, open-ended questions that can get them talking, like: "What's on your mind?" "What has troubled you this week?"

Provide correction — even though it might be painful. Confront self-defeating behavior but temper the confrontation with realistic affirmation. Address unethical, unprofessional, illegal behavior. Confront personal distress and negative work habits. Recognize that appropriate confrontation builds trust.

Be an intentional model. Let them observe you, but also require them to participate in an increasing manner. Display dependability — ensure you follow through on everything you commit to with the people you mentor. Be trustworthy: keep promises and adhere to professional and organizational codes. Above everything else, maintain confidences. Exude warmth. Radiate warmth with an attitude of friendliness, approachability and kindness.

Listen actively. Drop other activities when those you mentor want to talk. Give them your undivided attention. Paraphrase back to them what they just shared with you, to ensure you understood them correctly.

Embrace humor. And always respect values. Do not be neutral on values. Show your core beliefs and values. Count the cost, including expenditure, potential for failure and your time.

Mentorship and discipleship are closely related

It was Jesus who told us, *Go and make all people disciples... teaching them to obey all I have commanded you* (Matt 28:19-20). *Go and bear fruit that is lasting* (John 15:16).

As followers of Christ, we are to mobilize, train and motivate other people to be functioning, committed followers of Jesus Christ — to become like him.

Jesus spent time with the twelve. Paul invested in Timothy, Silas, Epaphroditus, and later, Mark. In the Old Testament, Moses trained Joshua, and later in the biblical history, Elijah trained Elisha.

Through teaching and practical application you are training at least three others, as well as encouraging them to do the same: Train three others in their turn. This is a biblical concept for both mentoring and discipling. As we are obedient to this biblical principle, the kingdom of God will move forward with great speed.

You have heard me teach many things that have been confirmed by many reliable witnesses. Teach these great truths to trustworthy people who are able to pass them on to others (2 Tim 2:2).

You are taking what God has entrusted and taught you, and by means of this simple guide, attempting to engage three or more people in becoming followers of Christ in every aspect of their lives. This can be done through learning some basic biblical, mentoring concepts and by taking some very practical risks for God.

Who do I mentor?

Anyone that God brings in your path: Your closest friends, people you know who really need a "kick," people in your church, believers you know through work, friends of friends, the people who lead groups in your church, or perhaps your kids.

How and where do I begin?

The best way to get into a regular mentoring routine is to set a fixed time in the same place on a regular weekly schedule. If you are a frequent traveler, you may have to be more flexible in your schedule.

I have found that it works best to meet for breakfast, lunch or coffee once a week, preferably on a weekday. By scheduling it as breakfast, you have a limited window of time before you have to be at work. Setting a boundary will help discipline your time together. Do not take up family time (like a Saturday or Sunday).

You can either meet one-on-one or one-on-three. For general issues, one-on-three will work well. There may be times that you also need to hold an extra one-on-one session, where the person you mentor can feel free to open up about specific issues that may be of a more private nature.

Meet in any kind of breakfast place, a coffee shop or even at your home or office.

Concentrate on the meeting and do not spend too much time chit-chatting about other issues such as work, family or menu selections. Allow no more than an hour for the entire meeting. Do not introduce more topics during the meeting than what you have previously decided to focus the mentoring sessions on.

When do I begin and when does it end?

A few years ago, I put together a twelve-week course for those who want to mentor others. I called it *Mentoring Risk-Takers.* If you are interested in using this resource, just send me an email and a mailing address, and I will send you four booklets, absolutely free. Place your request to Lars@dunberg.org. You can spread the course out over one session a week or more often if you and the people you mentor so desire.

After you have had your twelve sessions, you will find that a bond has been created between you and them. Then, it is up to you to decide if you want to continue to meet — perhaps less frequently, or one-on-one. Or maybe you will be at a point where you are ready to take on a new group of people to be mentored. You may also choose to have a break for a while. If you want to do it on your own, I suggest that twelve to twenty sessions with a set group of people is what you need. Then, after those sessions, you can decide if you need to spend more time one-on-one with someone in your little group.

Your mentoring impact

After a few months, you will find that most people you have mentored are eager to serve God and live for him. They may be wanting to take godly risks for the kingdom of God. They may also be eager to train others to do the same thing.

You will also find that the circle widens. You have just taken part in a concept of multiplication in God's kingdom. Perhaps someone mentored you with a few others. That person multiplied his/her impact three times. If you and your friends in turn mentor three, the impact is multiplied to nine. If those people in turn were challenged to do the same, there would be 27 of you. And if they in their turn mentored three, there would be an additional 81, altogether 120 people mentored and mobilized by one person.

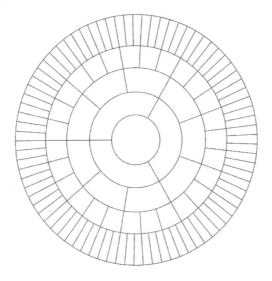

That's how many were gathered in the Upper Room for prayer, before the Day of Pentecost. Let us pray together that God may come and equip us with power and his Spirit in such a way that we become filled with boldness for God.

After this prayer, the building where they were meeting shook and they were all filled with the Holy Spirit. And they preached God's message with boldness (Acts 4:31).

Begin today. Either be mentored or mentor others. Perhaps you can find three who you can mentor immediately. Order your *Mentoring Risk-Takers* booklets now.

Jesus took time to mentor those close to him

Every student needs a teacher, and every leader needs a mentor. Jesus was a master teacher. He invested in and taught his twelve disciples constantly. Continually he taught them about prayer, heaven, hell, money, faith, purpose, giving, and relationships.

People may never see what you see or understand what you understand. You need to invest in their vision, their future and their purpose. Take time to train others.

Jesus did…and you can.

CHAPTER THIRTEEN
YOU CAN change your church

For many years, Stuart Briscoe pastored Eastbrook Church in Wisconsin, outside Milwaukee. In one of his recorded messages from 1985, he tells a rather funny story. Stuart was out grocery shopping, and in the vicinity of the cereal displays in the grocery store, a lady suddenly drove her shopping cart right into him. Staring at him, she burst out, "We left your church you know."

Stuart answered with a very non-committal, "Uhuh."

"Don't you want to know why we left?"

"No, not particularly."

"You weren't meeting our needs!"

"Have you found another church?"

"Yes, one that can meet our needs."

"Well," Stuart concluded the conversation by saying, "Next Sunday you need to stand up and make an announcement. Please tell the new church that you have come over to them to serve and not to be served. If you don't begin your season there with a new attitude, it won't be long before you push your new pastor against the cereal boxes and also tell him that you have left his church!"

Avoid the negative
There are two ways you can effect change in your church. You can impact it for the better or for the worse. Most available articles on this subject focus on the abundance of negativity among church members.

Why do people leave?

A new study by LifeWay Research has uncovered many reasons why some people stopped attending church. Labeled as the "formerly churched," 59 percent of those who left the church did so because of "changes in their life situation." According to the study, 19 percent of the formerly churched "simply got too busy to attend church," while 17 percent said "family and home responsibilities prevented church attendance." Other reasons explained were: moving too far from the church, work situation and divorce or separation.

Another common reason why adults leave the church is "disenchantment with the pastor and/or the church." The study reported 37 percent of adults cited this as a reason for no longer attending. Some of the factors contributing to disenchantment included the behavior of church members. LifeWay reported that 17 percent stated that church members "seemed hypocritical" and "were judgmental of others," and 12 percent said "the church was run by a clique that discouraged involvement."

The local church was designed to be a community in which the people of God can grow and flourish. Psalm 52:8 asserts: *But I am like a green olive tree in the house of God* (NKJV). When people who have been planted in a local church leave for any reason other than unavoidable circumstances, such as moving, it produces a time of grief for the pastor and for everyone who were close to them. The sense of loss, depending on the relationship the pastor had with the ones leaving, can be close to the feelings one has when going through a divorce or separation.

One pastor shared with me how, in the middle of a building program, a sizeable number of people left his church. Someone did not agree on some aspect of the new building, or how the building debt was being funded, and apparently spread their negative opinion among some of the sheep.

Some people leave because they have not established roots in the church. Without roots, people are like tumbleweed. They "tumble in" when they want, and then "tumble out" when they want. Very often, they take others with them.

Some people are simply running from the truth. When the Word of God is preached or taught, it brings with it truth and reality about God and ourselves. While the truth from God's Word should never be presented harshly, but in love, it should be presented and spoken. Correction should never be used to bring people to our own personal standard, but to the standard of the Word of God.

Eighty percent of the formerly churched do not have a strong belief in God, which the study indicated may account for the prioritization of work and family over church. Furthermore, among the top ten reasons adults leave the church, only two were related to spiritual causes, with 14 percent saying the church was not helping them develop and another 14 percent saying they stopped believing in organized religion.

The future is a challenge

Six in 10 young people will leave the church permanently or for an extended period of time starting at age 15, according to new research by the Barna Group.

Today's young adults are marrying later (if at all), are technologically savvy, and hold worldviews alien to their upbringing. Barna Research president David Kinnaman, after a five-year-study, declared that church leaders are unequipped to deal with this "new normal."

Positive steps you can take

Pray

Always begin by praying. It is difficult to be angry with or negative to a person you pray for. Begin by praying for the pastor and his or her family. For peace, for strength, for family issues, for dealing with the vision or the board, and for being able to prepare from the Word of God messages that will inspire, challenge and edify the body of Christ.

Then continue to pray for the elders, deacons and/or the leadership team. After all, a huge weight rests on their shoulders. They mostly deal with the budget, the finances, the facilities, and staff issues.

Pray for the worship team, that God will use their musical abilities, their choice of songs, and the use of sound and light in such a way that people will enter into worship through their leadership.

Continue to pray for every attendee, and for their families. Ask the church for a list of those that are sick or in the hospital. Pray for all of them by name. Finally, pray for the people who have been sent out by the church to serve those around the world.

Don't forget to pray for the people who will be reached with the Gospel and for the nationals that work so faithfully in their own culture and language.

Praise God for what happened last week, last month, and last year. You will be very grateful when you notice what God has already done in the church as well as in your own life.

Use positive instead of negative words

When I first learned English, I heard a phrase that I thought strange, and altogether untrue; "Sticks and stones may break my bones, but words can never hurt me." There are times I would rather have been beaten up physically, than having hurtful words to remember and mull over. Words can be very hurtful and can make a tremendous impact on your life. I still have scars from things people told me when I was less than ten years old. What you say, you can never take back.

What can you and I do about this? First of all, stop any and every use of insinuations, rumors and semi-truths. What do you do when people in church come to you and say, "Please pray for our pastor, he is going through some troubled times right now." If they add, "with his wife, or family, or elders..." they have made it even worse. Stop the rumor mill. Always say, "Have you talked to him or her about it?" Don't let it sink into you, and never share rumors with others.

Use positive, encouraging, confirming sentences. Thank people — not just the pastor, but everyone who works at the church. I remember working in one church where we tried to reach out to the youth that never went to church. One day, one of the older members came after me. "Why do you let these horrible kids play in there? Look, there are ball marks all over the wall!" Fortunately, another member overheard him and came to me and said, "Lars, I am so pleased you care for these young people. Attract them to the church as much as you can. I will come in afterwards and wash the ball marks off the wall!" What a spirit of encouragement. You can be that kind of influence in your church.

You can get involved as a volunteer

Every church is run by an army of volunteers. People are needed in the nursery, in Sunday School ministering to all ages, music groups, the cleaning committee, greeters as well as parking attendants. The church may operate a food pantry and/or a clothing exchange. Some night during the week there may be a planned visit to the local rescue mission, or even the local jail, and often the pastor will go alone. Perhaps some elder or deacon visits the sick, especially those in the hospital. That's just for starters. Find out who is recruiting these volunteers and go and volunteer your time. Tell the pastor that you can come with him one night a week. That will make such a difference, both to the pastor and to you.

You can become a great giver

It is always greater to give than to receive. In church, we tend to think more about receiving than giving. The average weekly giving in church, with all variables of age, location and size, is pretty dismal, approximately $37-$45 per individual. Take that times 52 weeks and the annual average giving per person is at best $2,340. If you are a couple, that doubles it to $4,680. If you are someone giving a tithe to the Lord, that means your average income as a couple for the year is $46,800. However, according to a census bureau report which was posted by CNN, years after the Great Recession ended, 46.5 million Americans are still living in poverty.

Some of those people may attend your church. When that report was published, in 2012, the median household income in the USA was $51,017 a year.

That means that if you have 100 giving units in your church, and your church is practicing tithing, there could be another $42,100 released for the mission of the church. I hold the view that in the New Testament tithing is not the issue, but generosity. The truth is that all I own and earn belongs to the Lord, and I can decide how much to give. Once you truly grasp the joy and blessing that comes from giving, I guarantee your giving will be much more than a meager 10 percent.

So, ensure that you give to the Lord's work through your church, not just out of your abundance, but sacrificially. Perhaps you could consider giving up five lattes for one week. If you have something with it, a scone or a muffin, there's another $25! Or, if giving up coffee is impossible, think of something else you could abstain from in order to multiply your giving to the church.

Encourage others to get involved in missions

One of the best ways to get other people in the church on fire for the kingdom of God is to encourage them to go on a mission trip with you. It has been proven that people who go on mission trips often become the prayer warriors, the givers and ultimately the leaders of the church.

So, plan ahead. Look at the websites of organizations that send out teams. Also, feel free to visit the website of the organization where I am the chair. It is called ServeNow, and the web address is: www.weservenow.org. You will never regret going yourself, and it is such a personal joy to encourage others to go, and to see what God will do in their lives.

You can break the generational gap

One of the major problems in churches of any size is the generational gap problem.

It is amazing to see all the different generations that make up the church. It seems that there are about 6-7 different age groups that are represented on a Sunday morning. You have toddlers and babies in the nursery, the preschoolers and kindergarteners, the elementary school group, and then the junior high age, followed by the high school students. If it is a big church, they may also have a class for college students. In some cases, these groups even have separate church services from the main service in the sanctuary, where the adults meet.

If that is not so, the students in high school and college may be part of the adult service as well. This is where some of the differences in personal preference come into play. Music is often at the center of the discussion. In the main, older people do not like loud music and, in general, younger people love loud music. The issue is not that black and white, but for some reason it seems to be that you have to land on one side or the other. The problem with choosing sides is that someone is always left out. Today, we see a rise of generational churches made up solely of certain age groups.

Be an advocate for breaking this pattern. We need to have services that include everybody. Young people today will benefit from the wisdom of seniors. In a world where there are so many voices to listen to, senior adults and adults can play a major mentoring role for young people. While there may seem to be an insurmountable disconnect between the generations, it does not need to be so. You can make a difference by bridging the gap, wherever you are on the generational scale.

We don't want a church filled with only people like me, or with only people like you. There is strength in every generation. Let us learn from each other and gain wisdom through each generation that provides a unique perspective on life.

Jesus promised that he will build his church. You can help him and he will enable you to do so.

CHAPTER FOURTEEN
YOU CAN equip a church

Have you ever given thanks for what past and present members of the church have provided, so that you can have a great worship experience?

If you are in an older church, that may have existed over 150-200 years, you can almost be sure that some of your ancestors, coming from the "old world," sacrificed greatly of their meager earnings to make the building a reality. They did not only bring their faith from the old world, but also great work ethics and a commitment to support the Lord's work with everything they had. In most newly founded villages, which later turned into larger cities, the first buildings to be constructed, apart from homes, were a school, a court and a church, or in many cases, several churches. If it had not been for the sacrifices of those immigrants and pioneers, the church would not have been there.

Perhaps your church is more of a traditional church, and the building was constructed 50-100 years ago. Many of those churches were built and equipped by your great grandparents — if you indeed go to church in the same community your family came from. Often the contributions did not only come from a mix of some well-established people in the church, such as bankers, builders, and owners of corporations, but also from regular hard-working people who gave sacrificially. From those funds, the church members had the building constructed, the organ purchased, and the pews delivered.

In today's more contemporary churches, Christians may meet in church buildings, in converted warehouses, or even crystal cathedrals. Whatever the structure, it took resources that someone provided. You may have been one of those providers. Today, the majority of the cost goes to chairs, carpets, high tech sound equipment, lights, coffee machines, screens, projectors, and the so called "pew" Bibles, even if the pews are gone. Some of these churches still have huge mortgages on their buildings, and you may still help provide funding for it to be paid off.

There are others that also need you

Since those early days of the first disciples, the worldwide church has continued to grow around the world. Local churches have been started everywhere. Life in Christ has been found by millions as members of those churches — the body of Christ — began sharing their faith with others.

We tend to mistake the church for the building. "I was married in that church!" we say. "I worship in that church," we explain, pointing to a structure that could be a cathedral, a traditional looking church, a converted warehouse or store front, or even a living room.

Many of the new churches around the world today are more concerned with community than location. More often than not, the new church is made up of a handful of new believers meeting in an open field, under a tree, or even on a garbage dump. It may take years before they ever have a building of their own. But they are effective. They share their faith with others. And often they split — not out of theological, ideological or personal differences — but because they believe that creating small centers of worship within walking distance from each neighborhood will make them even more effective in spreading the Gospel.

While you need to continue to support the ministry of your local church, including special drives for this and that piece of new equipment, I would encourage you to also consider those who are less fortunate.

Every year over 40,000 new churches are launched in the world. Many of these churches came into existence because someone went out into remote villages or into the worst of slums and shared the Gospel. Often it goes like this: one or two people in a remote area come to Christ and are given a Bible and a New Testament in their language. Contrary to how people in the West often want to keep their faith as a private matter, these new converts become very enthusiastic about their newfound faith and go around sharing it with anyone they come across. The result is that a group of people come to listen to these new converts on a regular basis, asking them to share more stories from that mysterious book they call the Bible. It does not take many months before a nucleus church of new converts is established, and the new convert becomes the pastor — full of enthusiasm, but knowing very little.

Today there are literally thousands of these new churches in almost every area of Africa, Asia and Latin America.

What can you and I do?

God's Word for God's New People

I want to see every church I can find in the Western Hemisphere partner with a project called *God's Word for God's New People*. It would entail placing New Testaments, in their own language, in the hands of these new believers in these remote churches, whether in distant villages or in the concrete jungle slums.

As believers, we would find it hard to even imagine going to church, living a Christian life, or being a witness for Christ, without having access to God's Word. We treasure our Bibles. We read them, study them, mark them and even read them through in different versions so that the biblical meaning will be clear to us. Here we are trying to give new believers the same privilege — to read and keep their own copy of the Word of God. For approximately $5 per person, we can design and produce a New Testament, bring it to these remote places and have an evangelist or Christian worker visit the church, teach these believers how to read the Bible, and then place it in their hand. The cost of a fast food meal — that is all it takes to equip a church member with what should be most precious to you and me.

The basic things you need to know...

Imagine having come to faith a few months ago. Your entire family is steeped deeply in the local religion and has never even heard the name of Christ. Your pastor is a fairly recent convert himself and has never even attended a Bible course. The other day, you received your first copy of a New Testament. However, when it comes to basic Christian teaching on the most basic subjects, neither you nor your pastor has much understanding at all. There is no Christian bookshop in the village you live in. As a matter of fact, there is no supply of books anywhere within several hundred miles!

There are some materials available to assist these new believers as well as their pastors, through a basic booklet series called *The Basic Things Series*. Each booklet addresses a key subject in the Christian faith. They carry titles like *The Basic Things You Need to Know About Jesus* or *The Basic Things You Need to Know About Salvation*. The booklets cover 28 different subjects.

Each booklet is 32 pages long, written in basic, easy-to-read language, using as little "Christianese" as possible. They have already been translated into the following languages: Spanish, Russian, and Luganda (for Uganda). For India the following translations are available: Bengali, Hindi, Nepali, Odhya, Punjabi, and Telugu.

Every three months, a new booklet will be available to church members, thus building a library of 28 booklets on a variety of topics over seven years. You may even use the same booklets in English in your own church. They can be obtained from the publisher of this book, Mountainbrook Press.

***

Here are a few stories from pastors that have already equipped their churches with the assistance of people like you.

David Vikash pastors a church of 60 adults and 40 children called *Mominpur House of Prayer*, in Kolkata, India. As a convert from Hinduism, he understands the power of God's Word. All the people in the church are converts from Hinduism through David's ministry.

He has not had any formal pastoral training. However, he has a passion for the Lord. From the day he received Jesus Christ as his personal Savior, he has had a vision for evangelism, and it is being fulfilled by those he has brought to his little church. The New Testaments and *The Basic Things You Need to Know About Jesus* and *The Basic Things You Need to Know About Reading and Studying the Bible* in Bengali, have been like gold mines for his congregation. Now he is eagerly awaiting the next two books in the series: one on *Salvation* and one on *Prayer*.

Khetrabasi Awaz pastors a church of 55 people in a village called Kaniha, in the Indian state of Odisha. Kaniha is an industrial area and also has a huge coal mine.

In his small congregation there are thirteen families who have come to Christ out of Hinduism and who have been baptized. Pastor Awaz is also a talented *Pala/Kirtan* (country/drama) singer, a writer and a poet. He has written and published several gospel tracts, which he and his church members have been sharing with the villagers, in an attempt to draw them to visit the little church.

Pastor Awaz knows the power of written material like this. He came to Christ from a Hindu family after reading a gospel tract over ten years ago. Later on, his whole family also became believers in Jesus. He began to share his testimony to people, and distribute tracts. Then, he planted a small house church. Now they have been equipped with New Testaments and have begun getting the first year's supply of the teaching booklets. To give these church members four booklets a year only costs $5 per member.

You can provide little things that are huge to them

As we minister to all these churches, we are faced with some very intriguing needs. Some of these needs are enormous for the people who are facing them. While they pray, they cannot fathom how

God will ever be able to meet these needs. Because we have heard about them, we have in turn prayed about these needs and seen them fulfilled. It is one of the greatest joys in life to be able to meet these needs. Here are a few examples:

One of the first churches to which we provided New Testaments and booklets was a church that is built on a garbage dump, where rag pickers and others live. So far the pastor has been able to lead more than 50 people to the Lord, and they meet in a building right on the garbage dump. When he understood he was getting all these study aids, he said it was as if angels from God had visited them. Then he shared his humongous need.

"When it rains, our mud floor becomes impossible to sit on, and the ladies with their saris find it hard to come to church. We are praying for ten bags of cement, so we can make a cement floor." Within days we were able to raise the $75 dollars it cost to provide the floor, and the church members are now praising God.

When asking a village church in a remote area what their biggest prayer need was, the pastor mentioned that there had never been a medical doctor visiting the village. Fortunately, *Serve-Now*, the organization that is providing the Scriptures and booklets, has a medical doctor on their board. It did not take many days for a doctor, nurses, staff members, and volunteers to come to the village and conduct a medical camp for a day.

At first, the villagers were reluctant to come, but soon they realized they were being helped. Over 100 patients were treated in one day. While the medical personnel saw to their medical needs, staff and volunteers prayed with them and gave them a New Testament in their own language. Now the pastor is welcome into every hut in that village, because through his help they received medical treatment.

In Uganda, the pastors are living in remote areas and often pastoring several congregations. Their biggest need is a bicycle, so they can get quickly from place to place. Recently we were able to place bicycles with several pastors. This was such an awesome occasion for them that they dressed up in their best clothes, some in three-piece suits, white shirts and ties, to receive their new mode of transportation.

Recent requests have varied from toilets in the church, musical instruments, a bongo drum and a guitar, and plastic chairs to sit on. Another request seemed a bit bewildering to us. "We need mattresses for worship!" Did it mean that they would sleep while they worshipped God? Speaking in a Nepali church in Hyderabad, India, I finally understood. There were thin mats laid out on the ground, and people sat on them. It was a long service. A soft mattress would make it easier for them to sit for many hours and listen to the message!

You can help train them

Jonathan Lima grew up as a nominal Christian in a small village in southern Odisha (formally Orissa), India, and moved to Cuttack about 15 years ago in search of work. For a couple of years, he worked as a rickshaw puller and then became a vendor for a local bakery. He was not part of a Christian fellowship, and he was miserable. Finally, he began to attend Sunday worship at a local church and realized how much he needed Jesus in his life. One night, in February 2002, he couldn't sleep. As he thought about how miserable his life was, he heard a voice saying, "Why are you so worried? Commit your life to me."

Jonathan committed his life to Jesus that night and invited him to come into his heart as his Savior and Lord. He told his wife and children about his new experience, and soon began to tell many others in the slums and streets of Cuttack about his new life in Jesus.

The Lord did a marvelous work through Jonathan. People were healed from their diseases, and they believed in Jesus and became his followers. He planted a small house church in the slums. Soon the small house could not hold all the families that had come to faith, and they had to move into a rented building.

As the church continued to grow, the struggle within Jonathan grew as well. Jonathan knew how to read his Bible, but he did not know what or how to teach his congregation effectively. Around that time, a ministry brought a teaching program to the city, and when he heard about it, his joy knew no bounds. He enrolled in the program in 2009 and graduated in 2010. He was very excited about the new insights he gained as he studied each module. Now he not only had the materials to help teach his congregation, but the skills to teach from his Bible. His congregation is encouraged when they receive proper spiritual food, and they are becoming stronger and more mature in their spiritual lives.

Today, Jonathan has one church and three house fellowships where he is involved continually in making disciples for Christ.

At the same time, in Ukraine, Sergey Udovidichenko had a rough life. For 15 years he was addicted to alcohol and spent time in several rehabilitation centers. But one day in 2003, he met Jesus Christ and his life was completely transformed. He quickly began to share his newfound faith and became an evangelist. To get some foundational training, he enrolled in a similar training program in Crimea, Ukraine and graduated in 2006.

At that time, Sergey was the leader of church evangelism in a church called *Love of Christ* in the city of Krasnoperekopsk, Crimea. Through the training program he was taught to preach, to do personal evangelism and how to relate to people in order to share the Gospel with them. It helped him to change the ways he had shared the Gospel in the past. Since he graduated he has launched four churches and has taught people in these churches using the same materials he learned from. Under his leadership, six people have become pastors and leaders of these churches.

Today, Sergey is a church leader whose ministry has gone beyond his church and the location where he resides. He is involved in evangelism in many other places in Ukraine and is helping others to start new churches. He is an evangelist who is always on the go to bring the Gospel to others.

Alexander Alexandrov grew up under the Soviet Union's philosophies. He considered himself an atheist. When the wall came down he worked as a private entrepreneur. However, one day he was threatened by the local mafia and had to give up his business. Totally ruined, he found himself in a desperate situation.

One day, as he was walking along the street, not knowing what to do, he saw a woman who needed some assistance. After he had helped her across the street, she turned to him and asked if she could pray for him. Through that prayer he heard for the first time that Christ's name could save him from his desperate situation. The lady invited him to come to church the following Sunday so he could be a part of a huge Christian family. The following Sunday he went to church, and was embraced in his newfound faith. That was in 1995.

He was already a pastor when he attended a training program in Ukraine, together with many others, and graduated in 2008. After graduation, he started a new church with ten people from the village. Today, this church has 50 people. His church has increased in numbers due to home churches planted in nearby villages. The area he works in is under the influence of the Russian Orthodox Moscow patriarchate. The villagers are therefore hesitant to listen to the Gospel from others, believing their Orthodox beliefs are all they need. However, the villagers have come to appreciate Alexander's sincere work among them. Due to his ministry, some of them have begun attending the home churches. The textbooks from the training program have been helpful for both sharing the Gospel with newcomers and teaching new leaders in these home churches.

It does not take giant resources to make a huge difference in many of these churches. The Lord is looking for people who are willing to think outside of the walls of their own church and invest in God's kingdom around the world. Jesus said, The harvest is great, but the workers are few. So pray to the Lord who is in charge of the harvest; ask him to send more workers into his fields (Matthew 9:37-38).

Jesus needs you. These pastors need you. The members in their churches need God's Word and teaching. You can equip them!

CHAPTER FIFTEEN
YOU CAN assist in launching and equipping a school

Many of us take education — the opportunity to go to school — for granted. It is so much a part of our heritage and upbringing that we hardly think of it as a privilege. Most of have, at one time or another, even gone to school reluctantly, especially on those mornings when we knew we had not completed our homework or when there was to be a test that we had not studied much for. But for most of us, as we grew and matured, and as our worldview expanded, the more meaningful school became, especially for those of us who had the privilege to go on to undergraduate or graduate studies.

Many people in the world do not have the privilege of education. They would give anything to be able to attend a school regularly. Why can't they? There are many reasons. In some areas there simply is nobody who can teach, or if there is a teacher, there may not be a school building to meet in. In other areas, children are looked upon as a major source of income. They must spend time caring for the animals or being involved in child labor to help eke out a living for the family. Or there are school fees to be paid, and because of that, school is out of the question for families living under $2 a day.

Let me tell you about two countries where schools are waiting for our assistance.

Enormous opportunities in Uganda

Children in Uganda are desperate to learn. Some of them walk barefoot to school, only to sit under a mango tree or in massively crowded classrooms in old barns made of bamboo and straw. In many cases, the teachers are not paid well and payment of salaries is often delayed. There are basically no school materials apart from a blackboard, and the quality of the teaching might also be disputable.

Most children are naturally curious and will instinctively search to find out what is outside the village. When this curiosity cannot be satisfied, and they give up, potential is lost. The future of Africa comes to a standstill.

In Africa, access to education cannot be underestimated. It is their *only* chance to make a difference in life. It is their *only* hope to get out of poverty. Education alone can enable these children to eventually change structures like tribalism, oppression of girls and women, and post-war traumas, all of which trap them in poverty. Education is the main way people of any culture are enabled to make the changes essential to social and personal success.

Illiteracy and other challenges

Illiteracy rates in Africa, specifically in Uganda, are the highest in the world. The school system itself is faulty. Children normally don't even go to school. Because women are considered to be property, used for bargaining in marriage, girls are seldom educated. Other factors as well, such as disease, economic issues, malnutrition and war, are hindrances to education.

Improving the lives of girls in Ugandan urban slums is a must. As an educated girl or mother, an active citizen and an ambitious entrepreneur, they can break the cycle of poverty with application of modern technology, like Skype, to talk to product buyers across the whole world. They can also use social networks, like Facebook and Twitter, to open up more markets and interest.

Despite their proven potential, many girls are still uneducated and become child brides, targeted sex workers, or raped and exposed to HIV/AIDS. The girls and the women in urban slums have to collect water and wood rather than learning to read and write. Many girls bear children while they are still children themselves.

Meeting a man who makes a difference

A while ago, I was thinking I would love to get involved in assisting schoolchildren in Uganda. In particular, I wanted to see the girls get to school and finish it. But how could I? One day, the phone rang in my office, and a friend from Florida came on the line.

"Lars, we have recently met a man from Africa who you just have to meet."

"No, I don't think so," I said. "I meet people all the time who want me to get involved with them. I cannot fly to Florida this week just because you want me to."

"No," my friend insisted. "You are misunderstanding the whole thing. If you will give him two hours of your time, we will fly him to Colorado Springs to meet you!"

"Well, that's different," I said. "Let me know when he arrives."

The next day, Moses Ssemanda Mbuga arrived at my office, and we talked— not for two hours, but for two days! His story was incredible and seemed almost too good to be true. A few weeks later, my friend Kyle Pewitt, from Oklahoma City, was heading to Southern Sudan, and I asked him if he could make a stopover in Kampala, Uganda, to check this Moses character out. He did, and reported back to me in the positive. "Lars, he is the real thing! I have never seen anyone work quite like this. His reputation is stellar!"

Rev. Ssemanda Moses Mbuga began with a desire and purpose to rescue the growing number of orphaned and vulnerable children in the desolate areas of Uganda. His goal was to raise them in better living conditions while establishing a strong foundation onto which they would build their future, impacting them with Christian values so they could be transformed into men and women who will positively impact nations holistically.

Moses lost his father while in his twenties, and being the first born of twelve children, he became the father figure at home, looking after his siblings and mother. Due to insufficient funds at home, Moses chose not to pursue college studies so that he could save money for his siblings and mother.

He earned money from fetching water from wells for people's homes, and many times he walked miles and miles just to collect the water and carry it on his head in big jerry cans. Additionally, he also made bricks so he could earn something that would contribute to the support of his mom and the education of his siblings. At the time, the entire family was living in a small house made out of bamboo and mud.

In the later years, this entire experience drove Moses Ssemanda to have a passion for vulnerable children and suffering communities as he knew first-hand what it meant to live in poverty as well as to be orphaned. This was the birth to a project called *Imani Milele Children*.

Today, there are eight schools, attended by approximately 3,000 children. The main school is in a suburb of Kampala, Uganda, called Lusaka. *Imani Milele Children* is focused on providing education for children from grade school all the way through university — or as far as the child's ability will allow them to go.

Imani also heavily encourages sponsors and donors to come and meet the children face-to-face in Uganda, spend time with them, play with them, or even go shopping with them, just as they would do with their very own children. Nothing compares to the experience of visiting an impoverished child and witnessing first-hand what goes on in their lives — and knowing you can do something real to help them.

Why will their future be so difficult if they are not helped? With the prevalence of starvation, malnutrition, HIV/AIDS, and simple diseases that often kill family members, many of these children are often hurt emotionally and physically and become afraid of the communities in which they live. It is not uncommon to hear the children comment after their term break that they would rather be at school than at home. When they are asked why, they say it's because they "eat more at school," and they feel "safe."

In February 2013, I received an urgent email from Moses. One of the schools was hit by a fierce rainstorm with such strong winds that the roof blew off one of the classrooms during school time. The children were scared and rushed outside to find other shelter. What was he going to do to fix the roof? A quick email to a few friends of mine, plus some friends of my daughter, took care of that, and within days the funds for the roof were provided.

Through Moses, we found out about many other needs, but we also discovered many different ways to equip these schools. Most of the classrooms are made of mud and straw. Inside, 30-40 students share their school building with thousands of termites who are gnawing their way through the walls. One day, one of the buildings completely collapsed. All that was left were clumps of mud on the ground, with straw sticking out. It was time to begin helping them with classrooms made of brick and with cement floors, so the bugs in the ground would not bite the children's legs.

The toilets for the schools are simple sheds with a hole in the cement floor. Recently one of the toilet sheds simply sank into the cesspool beneath it. Fortunately no child was in it at the time. We still need to assist with building new, better equipped toilets. And then there is the issue of education itself. Especially needed are schoolbooks, uniforms, and teachers' salaries. Faithful teachers teach the children out of love, but often have to wait for months to be paid. And the most basic needs are always there: Food and shelter.

Moses dreams of acquiring more land to make the schools self-sufficient with food. He dreams of trade-specific education: tailoring schools, computer classes, a carpentry school, and a school to train future mechanics. And I keep dreaming with him.

You can dream with us too, and you can assist in equipping these schools.

> DEFINITION: Adult literacy rate is the percentage of people ages 15 and above who can, with understanding, read and write a short, simple statement on their everyday life.

Why education in India is important

It is normally said that education is costly, but ignorance is costs even more. This is true — without proper education, people cannot get decent jobs and will also suffer the social stigma of illiteracy.

Every issue that our society faces is like a link in a chain. Each issue is connected to another, either directly or indirectly. In the chain of issues in India, the weakest link is illiteracy. Illiteracy gives rise to many other issues; poverty, unemployment, child labor, female feticide, population growth and many more.

A person aged seven or above, who can both read and write with any understanding in any language, is treated as literate in India. According to the census of 2001, the overall literacy rate in India is 65.38 percent. The difference between the highest and the lowest literacy rate in India is very big. The southern state of Kerala has the highest literacy rate, which is 90.92 percent, while the northern state of Bihar has the lowest with 47.53 percent.

Illiteracy in India is characterized by wide gaps between the urban and rural populations. The rural population depends mainly on agriculture, and the rate of illiteracy is high. The people in urban areas tend to be employed, and therefore more educated. Even amongst the male and female population, there is a wide disparity in literacy. The male literacy rate is 75.96 percent and female literacy rate is 54.28 percent. The social system in India promotes education for the male gender while the female population, especially in the deep interiors of the country, is kept away from schools.

What often happens when illiteracy takes over

What is the inevitable result when a country like India has over three million children living on the streets? The movie *Slumdog Millionaire* may have made the street children a popular subject, but the pain in the lives of these children is enormous.

Can you imagine a country with almost 18 million children working as child laborers? It is like the entire population of Florida! Or imagine that one out of every six girls will not live to see her 15th birthday? Despite a compulsory primary education, less than 50 percent of the children actually have access to education.

In India, there are approximately two million children, between the ages of five and fifteen years old, who are commercial sex workers. There are a further three and half million in that trade who are between fifteen and eighteen years old. Together, that is as if the entire state of Minnesota was made up of juvenile sex workers! Eighty percent of them are found in the five largest cities. Seventy-one percent of them are illiterate. They are joined by approximately 500,000 children every year, year after year.

We can assist these children, one child at a time

As I was growing up, there was one city in the world that was considered "the armpit of the world," and "the black hole," and while it often was called the city of joy, it was full of utter misery. It had been the capital of the British colonial rule, and the boiling pot of major clashes between Muslims and Hindus during the days of Mahatma Ghandi. It was in that city that Mother Teresa found her mission to work with the orphans, the destitute and the dying.

In 1996, God called a young pastor and his wife to start working in one of the Kolkata slums. At the time, there was no Christian work in that area. Many families lived under a tarp set up against a railing or held up by two sticks at opposite ends. Here a family would live through generations in the same spot on the sidewalk. The parents might have jobs as rickshaw pullers or street sweepers and would leave their children to care for themselves during the day. Many of these children would find some child-labor work to help bring in money for the family. Few, if any of these children, went to school.

Pradip and his wife Ranjana did not quite know where to start. The slum dwellers accused them of having come to convert them. The police harassed them, but they would not give up. They began with a small Sunday school with just a handful of children. Soon, they realized that none of these children went to school, so they began with a tiny nursery school.

Today, five teachers and two assistants are taking care of a school, running from Kindergarten to Junior High. The hope is that we can assist them to double the school over the next few years, because the need is endless. While we can provide school uniforms, schoolbooks, and sponsorships, the people on location ensure these children receive formal education. In addition, the children receive a nourishing meal every day. They also learn Christian songs and Christian principles through a daily devotional time. The school is sanctioned by the Government of West Bengal.

In Delhi, another couple, Allen and Vanitha, began working with street children in one of the world's largest slums, Sangam Vihar. These children often have parents, but they leave early in the morning to go into the city to be domestic help, shop assistants, street sweepers and auto-rickshaw or bicycle rickshaw drivers. The children are left on their own on the streets all day long.

In many different locations across this slum, Allen and Vanitha have been working for more than ten years. Sometimes as many as 1,500 children are under their care per week. One of the core programs, apart from teaching these children Christian values, is a program focused on teaching the children basic literacy, learning to read and write. Ten part-time staffers work with them to make this a reality. Some of the children get help in their studies so they can enroll in a regular school. Most of all, there is an investment in the lives of these children, so when they grow up they can find employment and a life free of crime and sex-trafficking.

We can equip them with textbooks, rent better locations to create greater consistency, provide a meal a day, and train the staff so their programs will be even more successful. Recently, we provided computers for a computer class. As children become more technologically savvy, even in the slums of India, we need people who can provide more laptops, and then travel to India to help with some of the training.

You can equip this kind of school by taking some small steps, like helping with the cost of food for a day, a week, or even a month. It may take a bit more to go on a trip to India, but it will forever change your perspective on life. Jesus loves the little children, and there is a place in his heart for these thousands of children in the Sangam Vihar slums. He cares. He wants you to care as well. You can provide education and equip these, and many other upcoming schools, in the slums of Delhi.

You can!

CHAPTER SIXTEEN
YOU CAN multiply your resources

Are you satisfied with what you have in your bank account? Have you put some money in a retirement fund? You may even own some stocks. You may think you're doing fairly well.

Dennis Jacobe, chief economist for Gallup, has stated, "Even as stocks have returned to lofty heights from their March 2009 lows, the percentage of Americans saying they hold individual stocks, stock mutual funds, or stocks in their 401(k), or IRA, fell to 54 percent in April 2013, the lowest level since Gallup began monitoring stock ownership annually in 1999. "

Eighty-seven percent of upper-income Americans — those making $75,000 or more annually — own stocks, as do 83 percent of postgraduates and 73 percent of college graduates. Men are more likely than women to be stock owners. Those aged 50 to 64 are the most likely of any age group to have money invested in the stock market.

Although home prices are declining, foreclosures continue unabated, and residential real estate remains in a virtual depression; 33 percent of Americans say real estate is the best long-term investment out of the four choices offered. This is up from 29 percent a year ago, but below the pre-recession 37 percent in 2007. slide 1 of 4

Americans are horrible savers. Every American saves an average of $392 per year. At the same time, total consumer debt is over $2.5 trillion. As of 2008, the average household debt is $117,951, and this includes credit cards, installment loans, home equity loans, and mortgages. Half of Americans die with almost no money. So, how do we multiply our resources?

What will you leave behind?

If you died today, how much would you leave behind? Calculate the net worth of your house, your bank accounts, your stock portfolio and your retirement account. It's quite significant! Or is it?

My father died in July of 2008. Do you know what he left behind? Everything! What can you take with you when you die? Nothing! There are no hearses with U-Hauls behind them. When you die, it's all gone! Or is it?

The pinhead and the line

Imagine a pinhead and a line. The pinhead is extremely small — just a dot. But the line is a picture of infinity — no end in either direction. Life here on earth is like the pinhead, and we try to cram into it as much as we can muster. People make bucket list after bucket list, trying to do everything can before it is over — before they are buried six feet under, with no hope to live again. What they don't realize is that life is not a pinhead, it's a line. Your choices during your life on earth have eternal consequences.

The taboo subject in church

Death is a difficult subject to bring up. Even people in the church have a hard time talking about it. Discussing this taboo subject is definitely not a good way to start a conversation. If I go up to someone and say, "I think I am going to die soon!" people often say, "Don't say that. You will outlive us all!"

Of course I won't. Death eventually hits us all. The statistics are rather telling: 100 out of 100 people die. Life is nothing but a preparation for death. From the first day we are born we begin to fight death. The mother does everything to ensure the baby stays alive. Despite that, the baby has already begun the aging process. It grows up, loses its hair, what is left turns grey, wrinkles come, and finally the teeth decay, the back stoops over and the legs can't carry it anymore.

Once, I heard an old man say, "I thought I had prepared everything: the will, estate planning, including leaving things and funds to my children, but I had left out the most important thing — preparing for eternity."

We are only visitors, strangers, and pilgrims here on earth. The time on top of the pinhead is so short. We should be focused on eternity instead. If we are believers, it is folly to live like we have to soak up every drop of this life here. The real reward is waiting for us, if we invest in the right place.

What blessings await you when people hate you and exclude you and mock you and curse you as evil because you follow the Son of Man. When that happens, be happy! Yes, leap for joy! For a great reward awaits you in heaven (Luke 6:22-23).

The son of man shall come in his father's glory with his angels. THEN he shall reward each one according to their deeds (Matt 16:27).

The reward you will receive at the resurrection of the righteous (Luke 14:14).

How are you doing in the market right now? Perhaps it is the highest it has ever been. But compared to what you have invested in the heavenly bank, it has absolutely no value.

During the summer of 2012, we thought we had lost everything: our home, our cars, all our material possessions as well as our memories. Close to 350 homes burned to the ground in one of the worst forest fires in the history of Colorado Springs. My wife and I were in Sweden at the time, and we heard on the news how several neighborhoods were being evacuated, but it did not seem that threatening. But then one morning the phone rang at 4.30 a.m. and our children informed us that a windstorm had swept the fire over the mountain range, and our entire neighborhood was engulfed in flames. "We are quite sure your house is gone," they informed us between their tears.

At that point, we felt helpless. There was nothing we could do but wait. We cried, and we talked. We thanked God for 20 years in that house. We looked back to the ministry we had started in the basement of that house in 1998 — a ministry which had grown to touch the lives of millions around the world. Even if we had lost it all, life had been a blessing.

But we didn't lose it all! As the wind lifted the smoke after five days, we found out our house was still standing. The previous year I had retired from ministry, but coming home that day, it did not take me long to realize that retirement was simply not an option. We prayed, "Lord do it again! Even if we are old, let us see your kingdom continue to expand in the world." That is the only place it matters. Where do you invest? God's eternal kingdom or your own earthly kingdom?

You might say "Lars, I am all for doubling my investment in God's kingdom. I am willing to go anywhere and share the Gospel, but I have no resources to start with." Let me tell you about OPM.

In the early 1980s, I had the opportunity to meet the philanthropist W. Clement Stone who was the prime leader of the Combined Insurance Company of America. As we were having lunch, I was talking to him about the struggle to find enough funding to run the ministry of which I was currently President.

"Lars, you need to learn to use and double OPM," he said with a smile.

"Sir, what on earth is OPM?" I responded.

"It's simple. OPM stands for other people's money!"

If you decide to go on a mission trip, convinced that the Lord has called you to go, you will never lack resources to do so. Why? OPM. Other people will fund you as you share your vision. The ones you expected to give much may not give at all, and the ones you didn't think would fund you, will give more than you can imagine.

If God moves your heart to help fund a mission project, you will soon realize that it is hard for you to support it all from your income. But as you share your burden, arrange a garage sale, or a concert, or a simple fundraiser at home; other people's money will surface to multiply your own investment into the kingdom of God. I vividly remember the young lady who returned home from having been on a mission trip to Crimea, working among orphans. Within a month, she organized a concert in her church and trained the young people to perform. At the concert she shared about the project she had just attended, and raised over $1,000 that could be sent to help with the next set of children's programs in Crimea.

You will soon realize that investing in God's Kingdom not only is a blessing for those who receive the funds you raise but also blesses you as the giver, and those others who will be encouraged to give because of you. You can make a huge difference when you catch the vision for what you can do by inspiring others to invest in God's kingdom. You can!

CHAPTER SEVENTEEN
YOU CAN can go beyond the fads

I grew up during some rather depressive years in the middle of the 20th century. My dad was out of work for a long time, and some other times he could only muster up small jobs here and there, barely enough to put food on our table. At the same time, I placed my parents under enormous pressure because I wanted some clothing that was the "in thing" during those days: I wanted a duffle coat. Duffle coats were made of a coarse, thick, woolen material, with fastenings made of wood and rope straps. The coat was knee length, and it had a bucket hood to cover your head when it was cold. Everyone at school wore one (or at least that is what I thought) — everyone except me.

At school, there were only two acceptable music styles — one from Britain and one from the USA. You either followed Tommy Steele, the self-made rock-and-roll star from Britain, or you were an Elvis fan. There was nothing in between. You were either one or the other, and if you met the opponents to your style during lunch break, you could easily be physically beaten up by the other side.

What determined all this? Something called "fads." The free dictionary defines a fad as, "temporary fashion, or manner of conduct, especially one followed enthusiastically by a group. In other words — an interest followed with exaggerated zeal."

Today, fads are everywhere

By the time you are older, you have seen many fads come and go. During one season, the mini-skirt was the fad. Ladies walked

159

around wearing what seemed to be broad belts, but they called them skirts. Then the maxi-skirt entered the scene, and everyone had skirts down to their ankles — a very messy type of clothing when there was snow and slush on the ground. So, to get elevated from the ground, women started wearing plateau shoes, which took the place of high heeled stilettos.

Even pastoral clothing at church is not immune to fads. Pastors went from the dark three-piece suit, to a blazer and slacks, then to baggy pants and a sweater, and nowadays they wear jeans and (more often than not) a t-shirt. And it is all done in the spirit of communication. What will come next?

The bracelet fads

Friendship bracelets were becoming popular in 1989. Seeing the fad, a church staff member named Janie Tinklenberg asked a friend who worked for a local company about producing some woven wristbands with the acronym WWJD. Why? Because there was not enough room to spell it out. The purpose of the bracelet was to remind young people of their commitment to Christ and to use it as a tool to witness to friends.

After a while, some Christian celebrities donned a WWJD bracelet, and the rest is history. The WWJD bracelet could be found in any Christian store, in any color, in almost every country around the world.

Tinklenberg, now on staff at Peace Lutheran Church in Gahanna, Ohio, belatedly obtained trademark for the phrase, but since it was considered public domain she did not receive any royalties. However, others cashed in on it. By 1997, Lesco Corporation, the company that produced the first bracelets, had sold about 300,000. Then Paul Harvey mentioned them on his syndicated radio show, and dozens of corporations rushed in to capitalize on a market that spilled over into WWJD shirts, hats, key chains and coffee mugs.

What would Jesus have done? Most likely, he would not have sold cheap bracelets. Loyalty to him goes deeper than a silver or gold chain with a cross around your neck or a WWJD bracelet around your wrist.

The newest bracelet fad is the Mend Mark Bracelet. It is a distinctive wristband designed with the purpose of resembling one of the five scars that Jesus endured for his people. The band features circular disks that are positioned at each side of the wrist. The disks are supposed to simulate the wounds that were instrumental in killing a king. The purpose of wearing this symbol is to emphasize the importance of his sacrifice and prompt us to never forget the role that it continuously plays in our lives.

So, have you been "marked?" That's the password to this latest fad. The Mend Mark is supposedly an innovative and distinctive bracelet that is designed to reflect the scars and nail holes of Jesus. Its broader appeal has been loosely defined as a bracelet meant to inspire and motivate wearers to live a life of service.

What if all these gimmicks have only served to drive us away from actually talking about Jesus? Have we resorted to selling rosaries, charms, bracelets and programs to keep the "Christian" brand going? Have we forgotten that the Gospel is the power of God leading people to salvation? No wonder converts today have to be reminded to remain holy and righteous by adorning moral tags and reminders. Somewhere, something has definitely gone wrong.

The 19th century British Baptist preacher, Charles H. Spurgeon, once said regarding false doctrinal practices, "I cannot endure false doctrine, however neatly it may be put before me. Would you have me eat poisoned meat because the dish is of the choicest ware? It makes me indignant when I hear another Gospel put before the people with enticing words, by men who would willingly make merchandise of souls; and I marvel at those who have soft words for such deceivers."

Books

Do you remember *The Prayer of Jabez?* A few years ago, that was required reading for anyone who wanted to pray for God's blessings.

The Left Behind Series? If you really wanted to know what would happen to God's people in the future, that was the series to read. Some people did not seem to realize that these books were fiction. While they are based on the biblical story, they certainly did not replace the truth in the Word of God. The *Purpose Driven Life* in all its forms became the fad program any evangelical church of good standing should go through — especially the *40 Days of Purpose* series. It was actually quite good. It encouraged churches to focus both inward and outward. The final days of the program ended up with a focus on mission around the world. I became so excited that I flew out to Saddleback, California, to ask how such a massive mission possibility was to be practically undertaken.

Meeting with some of the younger leaders who had been appointed to execute the fulfillment of the plan, I boldly asked:

"What will happen when all these thousands of churches are ready to put the *Purpose Driven Mission Plan* into action? What will you do?"

"It is very simple, Lars. We will go all over the world and establish *Purpose Driven Churches* in every major city of the world."

"Sounds fantastic," I carefully commented. "But what are the local pastors in those cities thinking about such a bold plan?"

"What do they have to do with it? This is our plan!"

With that insensitivity as the foundation for a program, I am not surprised I have not found many such churches around the world. It was a fad that did not take root the way its visionaries had foreseen.

Movies

In the 1970s, young Christian people found it hard to sleep after watching the movie *Thief in the Night,* which vividly described the rapture in a rather frightening way. Thirty years later, the *Left Behind* movies were released with the same message, only to be overshadowed in 2004 by Mel Gibson's *Passion of the Christ.*

There will always be new movies with a Christian message. Some take on a life of their own and get a huge following, only to fade away and be forgotten.

Programs

The church is full of new programs. If it worked in one huge church, someone writes a book about it. Then it has to be implemented in other churches. Sometimes it works and sometimes not, as the Lord seems to use some things well in some places, without wanting it to be duplicated everywhere else. I moved to the USA when many evangelical churches were using Dr. Kennedy's *Evangelism Explosion* program. Other programs have come and gone: Spiritual Gift Inventories, Spiritual Warfare, Weigh Down Workshops, Becoming a Contagious Christian, a long succession of evangelism and stewardship programs, and not too long ago, Promise Keepers. Do you remember the stadiums completely packed with men? The movement served its purpose, but it is now over.

For many Christians, these kinds of events or Christian conferences as such, are what Christianity is all about. Some church fads come and go, some come and stay. A few are genuinely harmless; some contain serious theological error.

Theology

I began in ministry in the 1960s. There were two major fads in those days. Many of The Jesus People had found the Lord in droves through an initial ministry on a beach in Southern California, under the ministry of Chuck Smith and others. Many of The Jesus People came out of a drug-infested culture and, after their conversions, they began traveling the world with their message of God's love, "feeling groovy for Jesus," exporting their worship styles with guitars and tambourines. Rejected by many adults, it caught the hearts of young people. Suddenly they wanted to dress in jeans, the girls wearing flowery shirts and skirts, while the boys attempted to grow beards and look like Jesus.

Soon after we were married, I started to work with Youth for Christ. The focus was on evangelism. We were dedicated to win our generation for Christ. The Gospel would break through to the world in our lifetime. We were focused on the ones "outside the church."

Then the Charismatic Movement swept through the continents, inspired by such books as *Nine O'Clock in the Morning* and *They Speak with Other Tongues.* Many churches formed small charismatic cell groups, and while it was only intended to group like-minded Christians together, it created splits. The emphasis went from outward to inward.

After a few years, this movement, which brought a fresh touch to many churches of every possible denomination, devolved into something different. The clear focus, in the beginning, had been on placing God's Spirit and his gifts in the center of the Church. But the movement developed fringe groups who added things to the message such as "if you name it, you can claim it," and "as a true follower, you should never be sick." Some began recommending that congregants spend part of the worship service doing "carpet time," that is, free-falling backwards and entering in a trance-like state while people prayed over you. That practice became a sign of a "higher spirituality."

In another area of evangelicalism, your eschatological position became the guiding star, and was even used in choosing people for positions of leadership. One year, I was interviewing for a staff position with a well-known Christian ministry and I had a meeting with the chair of their board. As we sat down at the table — before he had even introduced himself — he blurted out, "Are you Pre-Trib?" In other words, did I hold the pre-tribulation view of the end times? Today the pendulum has swung again, and in the US there is a revival of five-point ultra-Calvinism among young people. While some of these theological swings can be a sign of God's move and spiritual renewal, they tend to become fads when they either go further than Scripture intended, or become the only focus among many other biblical truths.

Mission

When I moved to the United States in 1978, the buzz word in missions was "hidden people groups." Churches went to extreme trouble to document the most remote people group they could find that had not yet heard the Gospel. While this was a noble task, the rest of the world was simply overlooked.

The World Evangelization Map came into being, and when I looked at my own country, which was famous for being one of the most pagan nations in Europe, it simply stated "evangelized nation." I could not fathom it.

There may have been one generation when all the Swedes had heard the Gospel, but that time is long gone, with a new generation of pagans being born every day. God has no grandchildren, and the task of sharing the Gospel, whether to open or hidden groups, is a monumental task.

Then, suddenly, the Window appeared. Made popular by missiologist Luis Bush in 1990, the 10/40 window represents people living between 10 and 40 degrees north of the equator, highly untouched by the Christian message. It combines poverty with low quality of life and a lack of Christian resources for the existing, native Church.

Suddenly, if you were not called to minister in the 10/40 area, or your church sent out Christian workers to other areas, your missions program was almost suspect.

Now we are into a new phase. A huge social problem, which in itself is horrific, has become the new slogan for missions. "Are you involved in anti-trafficking?" is the question. The answer determines whether or not you have a solid mission outreach program in your church.

I wonder if I will live to see the next fad in missions. In the meantime, I am trying to figure out how all these fads are expressed in the simple message of Jesus Christ.

Then Jesus came to them and said, 'All authority in heaven and on earth has been given to me. Therefore go and make disciples of

*all nations, baptizing them in the name of the Father and of the
Son and of the Holy Spirit, and teaching them to obey everything
I have commanded you. And surely I am with you always, to the
very end of the age.'* (Matt 28:18-20)

How do we recognize these fads?

Here are a few simple ways to recognize a fad. First, it promises to
address biblical truth with a new perspective. Any speaker, book
or video that promises to unlock some scriptural truth in a new
or creative way, is usually outside the realm of biblical theology.
Jesus is the Truth. There is no biblical truth outside the truth found
in the Bible.

Secondly, we come to recognize the latest fad because so many
people are talking about it. When people from hugely divergent
theological backgrounds embrace a book, a movie or some other
cultural phenomenon, warning flags should immediately go up.
The reason so many people can embrace a certain book is because
there is likely such a lack of any solid doctrinal content that no one
will be offended.

Thirdly, if the marketing campaigns attached to the newest
fad in Church sound like the marketing campaigns attached to the
latest electronic gadget or a new fast food dish from Taco bell or
Burger King, then it is probably not worth much more than those
things.

*Unlike so many, we do not peddle the word of God for profit. On
the contrary, in Christ we speak before God with sincerity, as
those sent from God* (2 Cor 2:17).

What can you do?

What do we do with all these different fads? Somehow, they seem
to have little lasting impact on the majority of those who participate in them. Of course, there are always individual testimonies
of people who were helped or brought to the Lord by this or that
fad. However, the fads that come and go through the Church have

very little in-depth instruction from the Word of God and there-fore contribute little to any believer's *growing in the grace and the knowledge of the Lord* (2 Pet 3:18).

Fads distract. Fads make people chase goals or things that can easily take the place of the power of the Word of God, and true fellowship.

You can be satisfied with the Word of God

The Word of God always helps us where we need it the most. The Bible contains everything God has determined we need for *life* and *godliness.*

> *By his divine power, God has given us everything we need for living a godly life. We have received all of this by coming to know him, the one who called us to himself by means of his marvelous glory and excellence* (2 Pet 1:3).

It seems believers today have forgotten to think about godli-ness. Some of the fads appeal to people's "felt needs," instead of leading them into a deeper relationship with Jesus Christ and the Word of God.

You can involve yourself with God's people in your church

It is easy for these fads to become a substitute for getting involved in the local Church. Don't get involved in such behavior. Seek out God's people in your church. Have fellowship with them, not only during church services, but during the week. Help each other. Share each other's burdens. Pray for one another. You can be a strong influence in your own church, while staying away from all the fads.

You can graduate from spiritual milk to spiritual meat

Too many Christians are unwilling to take the time to seriously study the Word of God. Fads often encourage believers to settle for "baby milk," when it comes to teaching. Think of it as eating spiritual junk food. However, you can graduate from the milk bottle to the steak plate!

Work hard so you can present yourself to God and receive his approval. Be a good worker, one who does not need to be ashamed and who correctly explains the word of truth (2 Tim 2:15).

If you explain these things to the brothers and sisters, Timothy, you will be a worthy servant of Christ Jesus, one who is nourished by the message of faith and the good teaching you have followed (1 Tim 4:6).

Rather than chasing the latest best-selling book or video series, you can immerse yourself in the enormous riches of God's Word.

Some final advice from the book that is no fad and never fades

We will no longer be immature like children. We won't be tossed and blown about by every wind of new teaching. We will not be influenced when people try to trick us with lies so clever they sound like the truth (Eph 4:14).

Be on guard. Stand firm in the faith. Be courageous. Be strong (1 Cor 16:13).

The words of the wise are like cattle prods – painful but helpful. Their collected sayings are like a nail-studded stick with which a shepherd drives the sheep. But, my child, let me give you some further advice: Be careful, for writing books is endless, and much study wears you out (Eccl 12:11-12).

So focus on the Word and on Jesus instead of the fads. You can!

CHAPTER EIGHTEEN
YOU CAN serve where you are

"I want to serve God," a young person told me recently, "but I'm not sure what God's will for my life is. And I'm afraid I would choose to do something that is not in God's will, so I am waiting until he tells me!"

"I would love to serve God," another person said, "But I understand that in order to serve God, I need to become a missionary and move to a country far away. I am allergic to malaria medicine, and I can't handle snakes and spiders, and I simply cannot learn another language! I don't even speak English well."

I have heard the same kind of reasoning at almost every youth gathering I have led in the last fifteen years. The apostle Paul has some wise words for those young people.

> *Don't copy the behavior and customs of this world, but let God transform you into a new person by changing the way you think. Then you will learn to know God's will for you, which is good and pleasing and perfect* (Rom 12:2).

> *So we have not stopped praying for you since we first heard about you. We ask God to give you complete knowledge of his will and to give you spiritual wisdom and understanding* (Col 1:9).

When Paul wrote to the Colossians he sent special greetings from Epaphras: *a member of your own fellowship and a servant of Christ Jesus, sends you his greetings. He always prays earnestly for you, asking God to make you strong and perfect, fully confident that you are following the whole will of God* (Col 4:12).

The writer of the Book of Hebrews states: *May he equip you with all you need for doing his will. May he produce in you, through the power of Jesus Christ, every good thing that is pleasing to him. All glory to him forever and ever! Amen* (Heb 13:21).

There is a misnomer that you have to hop on a plane and go to the other side of the globe to serve God. Serving God has little to do with the other side of the world, but it has everything to do with your willingness to go to the other side of the street. You can serve him right where you live.

> *For Christ's love compels us, because we are convinced that one died for all, and therefore all died. And he died for all, that those who live should no longer live for themselves but for him who died for them and was raised again* (2 Cor 5:14-15).

Who do I serve?

Those who are your family

Some of your family members, whether siblings, parents or children, may not be sharing your faith yet. Don't preach to them at every opportunity, but do attempt to serve them.

It could be practical things such as helping a child or sibling with homework, doing grocery shopping for aging parents, or just spending time with your family members. We are always so eager to do things, but simply being with people is also a way to serve them. Go and visit a grandparent or an old aunt or uncle in the nursing home. Show your family that you really care. Your actions of service and love will make them so much more receptive to the power of the Gospel, than your mere words. Your joy in serving them will make such a difference.

Those who are your church family

Have you ever noticed how many needs there are in a church? There may be some single mothers in your church who are struggling to keep a job and provide for one or more children. You could take that family out for a meal on a Sunday. For anyone who is struggling financially, something as basic as a home cooked meal or a visit to McDonalds can go a long way. Then, send the mother home to have a break while you babysit her children for a few hours.

Ask her what her biggest needs are and you will likely be amazed at the sheer number of issues that are troubling her. Some of them are within your ability to take care of by simply offering your services. Others may be more difficult, like the need to have the car fixed or to pay some major bills. But you can become her emissary and ask other people to chip in and help. Your good deeds will be remembered for a long time.

Some of the people from the church are in the hospital, or in nursing homes. Ask the pastor if you can visit them, share news from the church, and pray with them. Others may struggle with health problems or weaknesses that confine them to the home. They are lonely. You can be their "sunshine" spot for the week, simply by turning up to chat, or perhaps singing some songs or reading and praying with them.

Then there are the obvious ways you can serve at church. The hardest people to recruit are usually the nursery workers. The church needs a nursery in order to serve young families with children. You have an opportunity to impact young children for life. You could guide them through their first Sunday school class, or even become a youth leader. This way, you will naturally see some of the children progress through all their growing-up years at church.

You may serve as an elder or a deacon, or perhaps find a place on the leadership team. I do! If you can sing or play an instrument, the worship team is a natural place for you. If you are still unsure of how you can serve at your church, ask for an appointment with the pastor, or if you have several pastors, talk to one that you may know personally. Ask for direction as to how you can serve the church best. There are not that many volunteers in most churches, and they will love you for your willingness to serve.

Those who are your friends and neighbors

Think about your friends. Probably, some of them are not believers. No doubt you have neighbors that you know well enough to say hello to. You are not sure whether they go to church or not. And then there are those thousands of families in neighborhoods around the church you attend. They are also your "church" neighbors.

Start with your friends and neighbors who already know you. Simply ask them, "Is there anything I can help you with?" They may say, "What do you mean?" Then let them tell you what their needs are, and it may be that you can serve them well in some of those areas.

In your own neighborhood, or in the neighborhoods around your church, you can take a walk and look at the yards and houses. There may be fences that are broken or are in desperate need of paint. Perhaps there are leaves everywhere and they blow into a neighbor's yard. Knock on the door, and ask how you can serve them. You may be able to paint, take out the garbage, or go shopping for an elderly person. You can mow grass or trim bushes, or even help with their laundry. You may share a cup of coffee with them, and talk about the things you are passionate about. When they ask you why you want to do it, just tell them that Christ has touched your life and that he was the one that served us so much he gave his life for us. That is why you also want to serve. Sooner or later it will lead to a conversation.

Those who you don't know but would like to know

You may have driven by the local rescue mission or The Salvation Army center in your community and wondered what they do. They serve! These organizations are always in need of volunteers to come and serve, sometimes providing the most basic needs. They may need a hand with sorting clothes that have been donated, or serving food, or stuffing bags of groceries to be given away. They need you to come and serve.

If you live in a college town, you may have seen some international students in cafes, or just walking around. They are the loneliest people. They miss their home, their culture and their language. The only exposure they have to your culture is the local coffee shop and the classroom. Find out if there is a ministry in town reaching out to them. If so, ask if you can be of help. Invite these "strangers" for dinner or dessert. They will never forget you. You don't have to preach. Just show in a normal way that your life is different because of Jesus. Even if these students speak excellent English, any material in their own language is like a cup of fresh water to them. Find out what language they speak and find a book for them in their language. Eventually, you may want to give them a New Testament or a Bible as a gift in their own language.

***

Serving, for the most part, does not take a budget. However, it does take a willing person who wants to serve their Master. Don't think about what you can get out of Christianity and Church. It is not about you. It is not about meeting your needs. It is about you meeting other people's needs in the name of Christ.

> *For even the Son of Man came not to be served but to serve others and to give his life as a ransom for many* (Mark 10:45).

Jesus came to serve. You can serve too!

CHAPTER NINETEEN
YOU CAN improve the lives of orphans

In the summer of 2002, my wife Doreen, our son Paul and I were visiting several orphanages in southern Ukraine to determine what work we would be involved in. Just as we arrived at one of the orphanages, a group of small boys were sitting on their potties. Suddenly one of the boys pointed at Paul and said in Russian, "Are you my new daddy?"

This little boy had probably seen people come to pick up children for adoption, and wondered if it was his turn. There was both longing and pain in his question.

The Book of James spells out what our responsibilities are towards the orphans of the world: *Pure and genuine religion in the sight of God the Father means caring for orphans and widows in their distress and refusing to let the world corrupt you* (James 1:27).

How many orphans are there worldwide?

This question is hard to answer because data is not readily available. According to *worldorphans.org,* there are an estimated 153 million orphans worldwide. UNICEF and its global partners define an orphan as a child who has lost one or both parents. By this definition there are over 132 million orphans in Sub-Saharan Africa, Asia, Latin America and the Caribbean.

Of the more than 132 million children classified as orphans, only 13 million have lost both parents. Evidence clearly shows that the vast majority of orphans are living with a surviving parent, grandparent, or other family member. 95 percent of all orphans are over the age of five.

Every 15 seconds, a child becomes an AIDS orphan in Africa. Every day, 5,760 more children become orphans. Every year, in Africa alone, 2,102,400 more children become orphans. Orphans in the world today spend an average of ten years in an orphanage or a foster home.

Every year, 14 million children still grow up as orphans and *age out*, i.e. are sent away from their foster care, with no family to belong to and no place to call home. That means 38,493 children age out every day of the year.

In Ukraine and Russia, 10 to 15 percent of children who age out of an orphanage commit suicide before age 18. Sixty percent of the girls are lured into prostitution. Seventy percent of the boys become hardened criminals. Many of these children accept job offers that ultimately result in a life of slavery. Millions of girls are sex slaves today simply because they were unfortunate enough to grow up as orphans.

Poverty is increasingly recognized as an underlying cause of overlapping vulnerabilities. It has been estimated that more than two million children are in institutional care around the world, with more than 800,000 of them in Central and Eastern Europe and the Commonwealth of Independent States. But the global figure is likely to be severely underestimated due to under-reporting and a lack of reliable data. Many institutions are unregistered, and many countries do not regularly collect and report data on children in institutional care. It is often poverty, rather than lack of family, which leads to institutional placement.

What can we do?

With so many million orphans in the world, where do we start? How can we possibly hope to make an impact? This problem must be tackled the same way as any other problem — one step at a time.

Start at home

Right now there is a move among churches in North America to ensure that children do not have to spend time in institutions. Organizations such as Orphan Care Alliance have a vision for the body of Christ to lead the efforts of caring for the fatherless. Its goal is to keep children with their biological parents whenever possible, by offering assistance to families and children in the community. This assistance comes in the form of education, financial support, goods and prayer, plus time spent walking alongside youth who are aging out of the state's care. Orphan Care Alliance helps these older orphans transition into adulthood, and displays the love of Christ while serving families and younger children.

They also advocate for local churches and communities to develop orphan ministries. They educate Christians on the needs of the fatherless and provide opportunities to care for them. These are growing programs which strive to preserve families who are in hardship. They provide resources for families who care for children, as well as providing financial support to adoptive families.

If you are a family with children, or without children, do you have room for one more at your table, and another bed in which to place an unwanted child? It may start with foster care which can then lead into adoption. Many unwanted children in our own country are waiting for us to care for them.

Around the globe

Today it has become extremely expensive and difficult to be involved in international adoption. In many cases, parents also find that cultural differences are deeply rooted and can create unforeseen traumas sooner or later in the relationship between the new parents and the adoptive child. Of course, it is not impossible; it is just a very difficult journey to travel these days.

This should not discourage you from adopting, if that is what God has called you to do. He will provide every financial and emotional resource needed, if that is your calling. That said, there are other small ways you can improve the situation for an orphan, right now, today. Many orphan ministries have moved away from the traditional orphanage as an institution, with dormitories for boys and girls. Instead they operate their orphan programs, using a family style approach, with each unit containing a father/mother as "house parents" with a group of 7-10 children in each family unit. Staying in homes, even if they are built together, creates more of a family atmosphere for these orphans.

Some of orphans have no access to education and are often used in child labor. By working with ministries that provide education for orphans and disadvantaged children, you may find that what you would consider a very small amount of money will go a long way to changing the life and the future of an orphan.

In our ministry, *ServeNow*, we are often involved in remote villages where orphans are cared for by a relative, such as an aunt, uncle or aging grandmother who is able to be only marginally involved in the child's growth and development. These children roam the streets without schooling or health care. We take the opportunity to conduct health clinics for these children, ensuring that they have the vitamins they need and treatment against the common illnesses like malaria and tape worm. It does not take much, but it goes a long way.

In some of the areas of the world, where it gets freezing cold in the winter, many children, especially orphans, have no clothing protection against the cold. While it may be several degrees Fahrenheit below freezing, many of these children still run around dressed in nothing more than a pair of underwear. They have no socks or shoes. Their legs are blue because of the cold. Each winter, *ServeNow* provides socks, gloves, scarves, sweaters, and knitted caps, as well as a blanket to keep them warm.

The average cost to provide winter warmth for these children is equal to the cost of two Chik-Fil-A sandwiches. You can do that!

If you don't know where to turn, contact any of these organizations and ask them how you best can get involved: compassion. com, worldvision.org, visiontrust.org, globalaction.com, and we-servenow.org.

YOU CAN IMPROVE THE LIVES OF ORPHANS

There are orphans waiting for you to intervene in their lives. You can!

CHAPTER TWENTY
YOU CAN help prevent trafficking

Lured to a good job

Maria is a 30-year-old mother from Ukraine who left behind her husband and two young children to take a job in Italy as a maid.

The recruiters, who originally promised her a high-paying salary, seemed to be representatives of a legitimate employment agency. Maria says they gained her trust because they looked professional and convincing.

"The process I went through to get to Italy was very normal. Everything looked fine. There were two other girls with me. They were from the same region, but I didn't know them. I was going to Italy to work as a housekeeper. They had already told me that I would be working either as a housekeeper or in a bar washing dishes," Maria said.

Her nightmare began after she and the other women arrived in Italy and were met by several suspicious-looking men. They were human traffickers in the illegal global sex industry.

"After arriving in the city," Maria said, "they took us to a building on the outskirts of the city and told us to freshen up and relax from the travel. Later, they confronted us with the fact that we would be providing sex services. This is a shock for any human being. Escape from there was impossible. The windows were barred and there was the constant presence of a guard."

One man in the building told Maria he had "bought" her for several hundred dollars. He said she owed him money for the cost of the airplane ticket and would have to work for him until the debt was repaid.

For the next nine months, Maria was forced against her will to work as a prostitute. Sometimes she was forced to have sex with 10 different men in a single day. She was beaten brutally whenever she refused. And if a customer complained about her performance, the brothel owner added a fine to her debt — prolonging her sentence as a sex slave.

It was only when the brothel was raided by Italian police that Maria was freed from captivity. Authorities in Italy charged her with prostitution and deported her back to Ukraine.

It has been several years now since Maria returned to her home in Ukraine. She still has not told her family about her ordeal in Italy. She says she is unsure if she will ever be able to tell her husband the truth.

"In the beginning, the desire for material wealth was at the front of my mind, and family came in second place. But after what happened, my priorities have been reversed. What is important in life is family — my children and my husband — in spite of everything," Maria said.

Snatched from the streets

Weeks after her daughter was snatched from a village in a remote corner of India, Rabia Bibi found herself in the seedy backstreets of Delhi. With no money and little knowledge of life outside her village, Bibi traveled to the capital in a desperate bid to find her daughter. For weeks she shadowed police during raids on the city's shabby hotels.

Bibi said she had little choice after 17-year-old Ranoo, her youngest of nine children, disappeared without a trace on her way to buy food in West Bengal.

"Three fishermen said they heard my daughter scream inside a speeding car," said Bibi, offering the only information she had about the kidnapping.

Navin Haro, a poor laborer, was equally determined to find his daughter, 13-year-old Jyoti Mariam. In early 2014 she was taken from their village in the Chhattisgarh state in broad daylight as she returned from school.

According to the India National Crime Records Bureau, some 38,200 women and children were reported kidnapped last year, compared to 35,500 the year before. Human rights groups say the actual number is probably much higher.

For Bibi, each police raid brought more despair, as officers rescued girls around the same age as her daughter, but never her own.

Although both girls were victims of trafficking, their fates turned out to be very different. Ranoo was finally found by police, weeping but alive, locked in a dirty hotel room. Haro, however, discovered Mariam's body about one week after she went missing, wrapped in plastic in a hospital morgue.

Promised jobs in Los Angeles

The girls—some as young as age 12—were smuggled into the U.S. from their village homes in Guatemala. Their impoverished parents were told that their daughters would be working in restaurants and jewelry stores in California and would earn good wages that could be sent back to their families. Instead, upon arriving in Los Angeles, the girls were taken to have their eyebrows tattooed and their hair colored, and then forced to work the streets as prostitutes.

Human trafficking is nothing less than modern-day slavery. The most vulnerable people in the world are preyed upon and forced into prostitution, unpaid labor, and domestic servitude. The FBI is the lead agency for investigating violations of federal civil rights laws, and human trafficking is one of the top civil rights violation priorities.

In the case of the girls mentioned above, the traffickers duped the unsuspecting families, and when the girls—who spoke no English, and had so little education that they didn't know their birthdates or how old they were—arrived in Los Angeles, they were told they had to pay off debts of as much as $20,000 for being smuggled into the country. If they objected to paying off the debt through prostitution, many were told their families in Guatemala would be murdered.

There was less subtle coercion as well. "These girls and women were physically beaten and were held in apartments so they couldn't escape," said special agent Tricia Whitehill in the FBI Los Angeles Field Office. "Members of the crime family would sleep by the doors with knives," Whitehill added. "So not only were they physically held captive, but they were also under constant threat."

The slave trade in Africa is not yet over

The enslavement of the Dinkas in southern Sudan may be the most horrific and well-known example of contemporary slavery. Up to 90,000 blacks are owned by North African Arabs and often sold as property in a thriving slave trade for as little as $15 per human being.

Animist tribes in southern Sudan are frequently invaded by militias from the North, who kill the men and enslave the women and children. The Arabs consider it a traditional right to enslave southerners and to own slaves as personal property. In a detailed article by Charles Jacobs for the American Anti-Slavery Group (ASI), Jacobs recounts how a 10-year-old child was taken in a raid on her village in southern Sudan and branded by her master with a hot iron pot.

Child "carpet slaves" in India

Kidnapped from their villages when they are as young as five years old, between 200,000 and 300,000 children are held captive in locked rooms and forced to weave on looms for food. In India—as well as in other countries — the issue of slavery is exacerbated by a rigid caste system.

The International Labor Rights and Education Fund is one organization that has rescued many of these child slaves. The group recalls this scene: "Children work in damp pits near the loom. Potable water is often unavailable and food consists of a few chapatis, onions and salt. The children often are made to sleep on the ground next to their looms, or in nearby sheds. After working from ten to fourteen hours, they are expected to clean out their sheds and set up work for the next day."

A huge industry

Trafficking is a huge industry today. It is estimated that at any time approximately 2.5 million people are brought into forced labor, most of them for sexual exploitation.

Of those, 56 percent (1.4 million) are in the Pacific and in Asia, 10 percent in Latin America and the Caribbean, 9.2 percent in the Middle East and Northern Africa, 5.2 percent in sub-Saharan Africa, 10.8 percent in the industrialized countries (Europe, Australia, New Zealand and North America), while the remaining 8 percent are in countries in transition.

No culture is immune from these tragedies. People are reported to be trafficked from 127 countries to be exploited in 137 countries, affecting every continent and every type of economy.

The majority of trafficking victims are between 18 and 24 years of age. An estimated 1.2 million children are trafficked each year. 95 percent of the victims experienced physical or sexual violence during trafficking (based on data from selected European countries). 43 percent of victims are used for forced commercial sexual exploitation, of which 98 percent are women and girls. 32 percent of the victims are used for forced economic exploitation, of which 56 percent are women and girls.

Of those who are recruiting victims, 52 percent are men, 42 percent are women and 6 percent are couples. In 54 percent of the cases, the recruiter was a stranger to the victim, but in 46 percent of the cases, the recruiter was known to the victim. The majority of suspects involved in the trafficking process are nationals of the country where the trafficking process is occurring.

Estimated global annual profits made from the exploitation of all trafficked forced labor are US $31.6 billion. Based on the previously cited numbers of trafficked persons, this translates into an annual illegal profit of $13,000 per victim. In 2006 there were only 5,808 prosecutions and 3,160 convictions throughout the world. This means that, in 2006, for every 800 people trafficked, only one person was convicted.

Children are trafficked both within and between countries for the purposes of forced labor, prostitution, forced marriage, domestic work, begging, use by armed groups and many other forms of exploitation. Statistics on children are hard to gather and often unreliable. Children trafficked into domestic work, for example, are hard to document due to the privacy of the home and because such work may not be regulated. Children who are trafficked for sexual purposes are also difficult to document because this kind of crime is so hard to detect.

Evidence from the United Nations Office on Drugs and Crime indicates that more than 20 percent of victims of all trafficking, both within countries and across borders, are children. In parts of West Africa, the Mekong region in East Asia, and some countries in Central and South America, children are the majority of persons being trafficked. Of survivors identified in 61 countries, 13 percent were girls and 7 percent were boys.

One area

Ukraine and Crimea (now in Russia) is a source, transit, and to a lesser extent, destination area for men, women, and children trafficked for the purposes of commercial sexual exploitation and forced labor.

Women are forced into the sex industry, or forced to work as housekeepers, in service industries, or in textile or light manufacturing. The majority of Ukrainian male labor trafficking victims were exploited in Russia but also in other countries, primarily as construction laborers, factory and agriculture workers, or sailors.

About 80 percent of those trafficked in this area are "social orphans" who live on the street because their parents drink, use drugs or abuse them sexually or physically. Officially, many of them don't even exist. Their parents never registered their births, so the state has no record of them. "That's why it's very easy for human trafficking to take place in Ukraine," said a local social worker, Mr. Svystun, in Odessa. "You can take somebody who doesn't exist, so nobody cares. Some of them are 16 or even 18 years old, and they've never been in school," Mr. Svystun explained. "They cannot read even simple words." The homeless youth are all too aware of the human traffickers hunting them. "Street kids are very smart," he says. "They know everything, especially about dangerous places."

Some homeless girls cut their hair and wear male clothing to disguise their female forms. To look at them, you wouldn't be able to tell they're girls. Because it's hard to survive on Odessa's mean streets alone, homeless youth join gangs and rely on panhandling or robbery to survive. A charity that specializes in rescuing teenage girls from Odessa's streets, said, "It's highly dangerous. Trafficking is big business and the police officers are often involved." Corruption manifests itself in other forms. One social worker commented that state orphanages sold children. A Christian organization recently attempted to rescue a 15-year-old girl. "But she did not want to stop working until she had seen her next client. Her ninth that day," the social worker said. Later they tracked down the pimp. It was a teacher at her school.

And here's one more thing to consider

While the majority of human trafficking victims are from other countries and may speak little or no English, approximately 33 percent of victims are Americans. They come from a variety of groups that are vulnerable to coercive tactics— minors, certain immigrant populations, the homeless, substance abusers, the mentally challenged and/or minimally educated, and those who come from cultures that historically distrust law enforcement or who have little to no experience with the legal system.

We can do something

We can do something, but we have to do the right things. Some "trigger-happy cowboy" believers suggested to me that we should send teams to the brothel areas of the world, so they could rush in and pull the young ladies out. You don't have to have seen the movies *Taken* and *Taken 2* to understand that this would be a very quick way to shorten your own lifespan. This is big business, and big business protects its assets and will go to any level of violence to defend it as well as to take revenge.

We need to work as intensely as we can to ensure that the girls never get there. So, what do you do in areas of the world where females have a very low status, if any status, in society? It is not uncommon for parents to sell their daughters so they'll have money to feed their sons. The girls simply have no value to the family.

A long time ago I did not think it was my problem, but today I have a desire to find as many ways as possible to give those girls value.

What can you do?

Find out all you can about organizations and networks in your community who deal with this issue. The church needs to be at the forefront of the war on slavery. Organizations like these can teach you to look for the signs of a potential victim, young females traveling alone in situations that do not look normal. The traders prey on these lonely victims-to-be. Let us help them before it happens.

Ensure that you support organizations who are working in this area around the world. A good example is *Tirzah*, an organization working to prevent the slave trade in Burma: 20,000 Burmese women have been taken into the brothels of Thailand and 50 to 70 percent of those returning are HIV-positive. *Tirzah International* is educating communities on the tactics slave traders use to lure their victims and the ways women and children can protect themselves. *Tirzah* also trains Burmese women in sewing as an income source for their families. *Tirzah's* Ethiopian partner is providing training in income-generating projects for families so they do not fall prey to slave traders. They are also working to rehabilitate a group of girls who have been returned from slavery in the Middle East. Contact them at Tirzah.org and see how you can be involved.

ServeNow is working in the slums of India to give young ladies value so they will be less vulnerable to the lures of sex traders. Through tailoring schools, these ladies learn a trade and can earn income. Others go through cosmetology school and find that in addition to providing an income for themselves, they can start beauty salons and employ other ladies who in turn, they can train and defend from traffickers. In this way, they are of more value to their parents than they would be if sold for a one-time sum of money.

Ukraine, and Crimea (now part of Russia), are sources of trans-national trafficking, where innocent women and children are being used for the purposes of commercial sexual exploitation and, in some cases, forced labor.

The girls we are trying to help are living in remote villages

The standard of living in remote villages in Crimea is far below that of the cities, and the poverty in those villages is severe. Being remote from any major cities make people unaware of the possibility of employment.

Because of such high unemployment, there is low public awareness about the dangers of antisocial phenomena, as well as lack of knowledge about available legal frameworks that exist within Crimea. At least 40 percent of every household has severe alcohol problems, exposing the girls to every form of physical, emotional, and sexual abuse. *ServeNow* is also trying to find a way to stop the flow of young teenagers into the trafficking stream from these remote areas in Crimea. A test program will take place during the next two years. The target group will be 50 teenagers from four villages in Crimea. The ages of the girls will be between 13 -15. If we start to work with this age, it will give us the opportunity to work with them for two years until they finish school. After school, some of them will make an effort to find work right away, while others will be forced to go to the big cities to continue their education. At that point, both groups are at high risk for entering into trafficking and prostitution.

ServeNow aims to help young people make the right choices for their lives, to show them a good example. With the help of local staff, *ServeNow* wants to instill Christian values in them, introduce them to Christ, and prevent them from getting involved in alcoholism, drug abuse, trafficking, smoking, and other negative habits which can ruin their lives.

Currently, the school is the center of life for young people in these villages. Therefore, *ServeNow* has planned to renovate and equip a separate classroom in each village school where the teenagers can "hang out" and meet project leaders.

This is an ideal program for anyone who wants to start helping victims of trafficking. You can support a girl in one of these schools. You can even go on a mission trip to visit them. Contact weservenow.org for more information.

Can we stop all trafficking? No, that is not likely. But every time we hinder one person from getting involved, that is one person saved from a horrendous life. We cannot do everything. But we can do something.

Jesus did not speak to all prostitutes when he walked on earth. But the ones he did talk to had their lives transformed. He lives in you. You can prevent trafficking— one person at a time.

CHAPTER TWENTY-ONE
YOU CAN be a Risk-Taker for God

In a world where Christians are being deliberately targeted and attacked, kidnapped and killed, dare we venture from the comparative safety of our comfort zones? Won't that make us easy targets too? It's more convenient to "stay put" and not ruffle feathers. But the God of Israel, who was with David when he faced Goliath, is also our God. The God who gave power to the early church is still alive and active today. He is not taken by surprise. Nor is he wringing his hands in despair, wondering what to do. But he does look for risk-takers willing to blaze a trail toward the ultimate victory that is assured — the day when *every knee will bow ... and every tongue will confess that Jesus Christ is Lord* (Phil 2:10-11).

We are surrounded by risk-takers

I felt amazement mingled with horror as I watched the sickening drama of September 11, 2001, unfold on television. Having been trained as a firefighter in my youth, I knew the incredible challenges those in downtown Manhattan were facing. Entering buildings and running up stairs to rescue the injured and evacuate as many as possible, they willingly took enormous risks — including the possibility of losing their own lives to save others. They were willing to risk their own lives for people they didn't even know. For many of them, death was the result of their heroism.

There are many types of risk. In another context, people often invest heavily in companies or individuals who seemingly can do no wrong. Employees trust these companies with their retirement

191

savings. Others follow the recommendations of stockbrokers and friends to invest in something that appears to be rock solid and safe, with sure-fire profitability. But with an unexpected and surprising collapse of one of these companies or trusted individuals, as a result of recklessness or deception, investors realize, too late, that the risks they took were very dangerous.

These are two totally different kinds of risk-takers. Here we will look at what it means to be a risk-taker for God. When there's a divine dimension to risk-taking, it can be the threshold of immense blessing.

Risks in the eyes of a child

Before getting any further into the subject, let me share something that came my way recently. It shows how children view risks somewhat differently from adults. School children in Boston were asked to write down some of the things they had learned about risk. Here's a selection:

- Never trust your dog to watch your food.
- Never tell your mom her diet is not working.
- When your mom is mad at your dad, don't let her brush your hair.
- You cannot hide a piece of broccoli in a glass of milk.
- If you want a kitten, start out by asking for a horse.
- Permanent felt tip markers are not good to use as lipstick.
- When you get a bad grade in school, show it to your mom when she is on the phone.
- Never try to baptize a cat.

Past pioneers were often risk-takers

History records countless pioneering risk-takers. In medical research, an English physician born in the 16th century risked his entire reputation on the true nature of blood circulation and the function of the heart as a pump. William Harvey was ridiculed for challenging what had been "established knowledge" for centuries. But because of his courage to take that risk, we all benefit.

A 19th century Frenchman called Louis Pasteur, risked his health and reputation to prove there are germs. Mainly known for originating the process of pasteurization, he also proved that micro-organisms cause fermentation and disease. He discovered a vaccine against anthrax and an antidote for rabies. His discoveries are protecting us against a variety of diseases today, and all because he was willing to leave the comfort zone of established medical practice and take risks.

German meteorologist and geophysicist Alfred Wegener was almost dismissed as a lecturer at the University of Hamburg for suggesting that the world's continents move about on great tectonic plates. But as a result of risking his reputation, he opened the gateway to greater knowledge of earthquakes and other geophysical phenomena.

To escape persecution in England, a group of 16th century Christians convinced a London stock company to finance their voyage to America where they expected a better life and religious freedom. We remember them as the Pilgrim Fathers whose risky transatlantic journey and subsequent survival set an example of immense courage for us all.

Again, history records that on July 2, 1776, the Continental Congress voted in favor of the resolution that "these United Colonies are, and of right ought to be, free and independent States." Two days later, the Declaration of Independence was adopted without dissent. On August 2, a parchment copy was presented to Congress for signatures, and most of the 56 men whose names are now on it, signed it that day. They took a great risk — signing such a document was to commit an act of treason punishable by death.

While some of those signatories went on to great political achievement, and two even became presidents of the United States, others suffered for having taken a risk for the new nation. Five were captured by the British, 18 had their homes looted and burned down by the enemy, two were wounded in battle, and some had their properties plundered. But what would have happened if they had not taken the risk?

Bible translators were often risk-takers

John Wycliffe is a good example of a Christian risk-taker. He lived almost 200 years before the Reformation, but his beliefs and teachings closely matched those of Luther, Calvin and other Reformers. This 14th century risk-taker challenged abuses and false teachings in the Church. What's more, he risked translating the New Testament into English.

The Church expelled him from his teaching position at Oxford, and the Archbishop of Canterbury wrote, "This pestilent and most wicked John Wycliffe, a child of the old devil, has crowned his wickedness by translating the Scriptures into the mother tongue."

But Wycliffe was convinced that ordinary people could not know the basis of their faith unless they knew the Bible, and that could only be accomplished if the Bible was written in their every-day language.

Forty-four years after he died, the pope ordered his bones to be exhumed and burned. Intense persecution stamped out his followers and teachings. But hundreds of years later, men like Martin Luther resurrected and built on the reforms of which John Wycliffe dreamed. And they carried on the Bible "revolution" that he started.

Similarly, William Tyndale, born in Britain some 160 years later, broke with tradition by proclaiming that God's Word is the only measuring stick for the Christian life. He revolutionized the attitude of the Church toward Scripture. He proclaimed, "The Bible to all — even to the simplest ploughboy."

Tyndale had to flee the Church and the king of England. Hiding in Antwerp, Belgium, he continued translating until his first New Testament was published in 1526. It was smuggled into Britain inside loaves of bread, baskets, barrels, and even in ladies' underwear!

Before completing the translation of the Old Testament, he was captured. Betrayed by a friend, Tyndale was arrested in Brussels, Belgium, and found guilty of treason and heresy against the

Church. He was executed through strangulation and his body was burned. But Tyndale's translation became the model for many subsequent English Bible translations.

Because these men were willing to take enormous risks, the English-speaking world is blessed with access to the Bible today.

Missionaries have often been risk-takers

A cobbler by trade, William Carey served as a lay pastor in Moulton, England, where he came to a clear understanding of the need for obedience to Jesus' Great Commission to go to the entire world with the Gospel. But when he shared his vision with other ministers, one of them simply replied, "Young man, sit down; when God pleases to convert the heathen, he will do it without your aid or mine."

Carey was undeterred, and continued to read, study and encourage people for missions. His motto was: *Expect great things from God. Attempt great things for God.*

He followed this when he sailed to Calcutta, India in 1793, never to return to his homeland. He risked his family (his wife and several of his children died there), his reputation, his comfort and his future. But, as a result of that risk, he translated the Bible and parts of it into 35 different Indian languages. He also provided grammar text books in seven languages, dictionaries in six other languages, and founded the Agricultural Society of India, as well as Calcutta's first daily newspaper.

No wonder he is known as the "Father of Modern Missions," and has inspired thousands to follow him in risk-taking obedience to the Great Commission.

Amy Carmichael, born in 1867 in Northern Ireland, became a missionary in southern India. There, she adopted over 2,000 children who had been given to the temples at birth to become temple prostitutes. Sometimes the mother gave the baby girl to Amy rather than the Hindu priests. Other times she simply stole them from the temple.

The Hindu nationals often charged Amy with kidnapping and constantly threatened her with physical violence. Sometimes they kidnapped the babies back again. But by far the most painful opposition was from the missionary community. They even questioned whether temple children were a "figment of Amy's imagination." When it was finally proved that the temple children were one of the best-kept secrets of the temple and that the government protected them, the missionary community said that Amy should not be so involved with "humanitarian efforts."

Risk-taking can be scary!

You may say, "But these people were great heroes, and I'm just an ordinary person. Surely, risk-taking is not for me!"

Fear of failure often hinders us from becoming risk-takers, even though we may suspect that life holds more excitement and satisfaction when we're willing to expand our comfort zones, try new things, and dare to achieve our dreams.

We may say we want to know the will of God, but when we find out what that is, we cannot handle it. It sounds too scary, too difficult. So we decide to look elsewhere.

People who are prone to focus on the negatives in their lives, rather than on God, often offer a variety of excuses. These include:

"I'm too old."

"I'm not good enough."

"My health is too bad." "It will never work out."

Problems may well come, but the results can be different than expected. It all depends on perspective. Results envisioned from taking a risk may turn out to be something better than we dreamed.

God uses ordinary people. The Bible is full of characters like us, people of both sexes, in a variety of professions, young as well as old, who were called to take risks for God. When they responded to the challenge, their lives were transformed and the impact is felt still today.

Risk-takers in the Bible look a lot like you and me

One young man was ridiculed and gossiped about by his relatives, brutally separated from his family, and later placed in a compromising situation with his boss' wife. He risked his life in order to be faithful to his God and eventually became the right-hand man to the ruler of Egypt. His name was Joseph.

Rahab was notorious for being a woman who gave into her sensuous feelings and engaged in promiscuous sex. But she risked hiding Israelite spies who came from Egypt to Jericho, where she lived. Her risky action led to Joshua and the Israelites conquering Jericho, and entering the Promised Land. Consequently, she and her family were rescued.

A young farmer's son called Gideon struggled with cynicism over what had happened because of the behavior of his father's generation. Depressed because he was not popular among the young people, he didn't believe anything could change his circumstances. But, challenged to take a risk for God with his divine presence guaranteed, he became an overnight hero and was placed in charge of his people for some 40 years.

At a time when women were constantly abused by their husbands and seen by other men as sex-objects, Deborah risked becoming a prophetess by telling her people the truth from God. She was so effective that the military general Barak even refused to go to battle without her.

Another woman was married to an immigrant, but, after a short time of happy marriage, her husband died. It was a time of crisis in her country. No jobs, no money and eventually no food. Ruth took the risk of becoming an immigrant in reverse, following her mother-in-law to her former husband's country. It took courage to change her country, culture and familiar surroundings. But her risky move resulted in finding another husband who provided for her. Eventually, she became grandmother to one of Israel's most famous kings, David, the great psalmist.

David grew up as the youngest boy with seven older brothers. They thought he was so insignificant that when anything important happened, he was not even invited home from his shepherding duties. In that solitude, David learned what it meant to rely on the Lord for strength and comfort. When the enemy threatened his nation, he was sent to the battlefield, not to fight, but to deliver packed lunches of grain, bread and cheese to his brothers. Upon arrival at the camp, he recognized that the greatest enemy threat was the enormous Goliath, who came out daily to ridicule Israel and their God. The young lad took an enormous risk facing Goliath, armed only with a slingshot and five stones. But his risk resulted in the enemies being defeated, and eventually David became sovereign over the entire kingdom.

Jeremiah was a young man when God called him to be his spokesman. Jeremiah's reaction was that he was too young to speak for God, and he shied away. But eventually he realized that the only thing worthwhile in life is to be obedient in service to God, even if it involves risk-taking. He said, *if I say, 'I will not mention him or speak any more in his name,' his word is in my heart like a fire, a fire shut up in my bones. I am weary of holding it in; indeed, I cannot* (Jer 20:9).

Jeremiah took the risk of being a proclaimer, which led to persecution, imprisonment and eventual death. But thousands of years later, we still remember him as a great prophet.

Another Old Testament risk-taker was a farmer's son, a young plowboy named Elisha. He was so insignificant that when the plowing teams went out, he was placed at the far back, behind the rest. One day, a prophet walked by the field and threw his cloak over him. Elisha promptly sacrificed his team of oxen and the plow to the Lord, leaving everything to follow the prophet Elijah. As a result, he received a "double portion" of power, and took over the prophet's responsibility as the conscience of the nation.

Joseph of Arimathea was an aristocrat of great heritage, wealth, status, and learning. But when Jesus was crucified, this man took an enormous risk! He identified himself with the dead "criminal" by asking for his body so he could bury him. He and Nicodemus, another secret believer, openly confessed their faith in Jesus as the Son of God. We never hear of them again!

Three fishermen, whose physically demanding occupation was low on the social scale, responded to Jesus' call to be "fishers of people." It was a risky move to leave their nets and boats behind. Peter, James and John relinquished their source of income and left their families to follow Jesus. For three years they were with him and, after the day of Pentecost, were natural leaders in the establishment of the early church.

A despised government official, the tax collector Matthew, responded to Jesus' invitation to follow him. By getting up and leaving his lucrative position, he risked everything.

Joanna and Susanna were two wealthy women who left their families behind to follow Jesus. They took many risks. For women to travel with a group of men was not acceptable in those days. Joanna's husband managed King Herod's household. Both risked their wealth by using their financial resources to support Jesus and his disciples, making it possible for them to stay on the road.

Then there were Aquila and Priscilla, who were tent-makers and lay preachers. In Romans 16:3-4, Paul writes, *Greet Priscilla and Aquila. They have been co-workers in my ministry for Christ Jesus. In fact, they risked their lives for me. I am not the only one who is thankful to them; so are all the Gentile churches.*

Epaphroditus was one of the "unknowns" in the early church, one of many young men who were messengers between the churches and the apostles. In Philippians 2:25-30, Paul writes, *I thought I should send Epaphroditus back to you. He is a true brother, a faithful worker, and a courageous soldier... he was very distressed that you heard he was ill. And he surely was ill; in fact he almost died... Welcome him with Christian love and with great joy, and be sure to honor people like him. For he risked his life for the work of Christ, and he was at the point of death while trying to do for me the things you couldn't do because you were far away.*

Timothy was a young man with an inferiority complex. Normally he would not have been noticed. But because he was willing to take risks in proclaiming the Gospel, two books of the New Testament bear his name.

Paul persecuted Christians and cursed their cause before becoming an enormous risk-taker after his conversion. In one place, government officials shut all the escape routes to capture him. But with the help of a basket and rope, he fled over the city wall, being eased down by similarly risk-taking believers. Paul almost always had to take risks to proclaim Jesus.

Risk-takers are those willing to go against the norm and get out of their comfort zone.

The Early Church was made up of risk-takers

At the beginning of the Book of Acts, Jesus and his followers already had different ideas about the best way to proceed. *They asked him, 'Lord, are you at this time going to restore the kingdom to Israel?'* (Acts 1:6). But in their minds they were thinking, "Lord, this is really exciting. Everyone is going to see that you're the king any minute now... right?"

Their focus was on the present situation of their nation and on what they thought Jesus would do. But his reply indicated a different focus: You will be my witnesses in Jerusalem, and in all Judea and Samaria, and to the ends of the earth (Acts 1:8). The disciples were looking for comfort and resolution; Jesus was pushing for risk and ambiguity.

There is risk in leaving the comfort of a safe environment

The Church's evangelism began in Jerusalem, and for a time everything went well. Thousands were saved and the world's first mega-church was formed, first with 3,000 members, then with 5,000.

Then an unbelievable tragedy happened. Stephen, one of their brightest and best, was opposed in his preaching by the authorities. Brought to trial, he preached an inflammatory sermon and was subsequently put to death. The effect of this was that everyone left the city, with the exception of the apostles. They stayed with the Church in Jerusalem.

While the disciples may have feared that this was the beginning of the end for the Church, the Spirit knew that it was only the end of the beginning, thereby fulfilling the words of Jesus.

As the disciples scattered because of the persecution, it seems that the disciples "went everywhere and gossiped the Gospel." Despite what had happened to Stephen, they were still willing to take risks, and to take the Gospel outside their comfort zone of the very first church.

There is risk in reaching out to people who are different

If Jesus' first area of concern was Jerusalem, his second was Judea and Samaria. Rumor reached Jerusalem that Philip had gone and preached in Samaria, and that some Samaritans had become believers in Jesus, but with no evidence of the Holy Spirit being present.

Imagine the conversation at the church office in Jerusalem: "No Holy Spirit? They simply can't be real believers. Becoming a disciple means receiving the Spirit. To be honest, I'm not convinced that Samaritans can be disciples anyway. There always was something strange about them and their religion. Everyone knows that."

Peter and John were sent to check it out. Even after three years of being around Jesus, watching him challenge one religious tradition after another, they were still nervous when it came to doing the same.

God seemed to be pushing these church leaders into new risks: "Notice what's happening here," he seemed to be saying, "Never forget it. The Gospel is for everyone, even Samaritans!"

There is risk in the seemingly insignificant

As Philip continued his fruitful evangelistic ministry in one Samaritan city, hundreds came to faith, dozens were healed, and demons fled in terror. A little scary — but very exciting!

One morning, the evangelist simply announced he had to leave. To go and preach to bigger crowds? No, just the opposite. God had called him to leave the crowds and the success of his ministry to go take a walk on a desert road in Gaza. Then, God surprised even Philip with a divine appointment.

Ethiopia's finance minister, who identified himself with the Jewish religion, was the only man traveling on that otherwise deserted road at that particular moment. He had just fulfilled a long-time ambition to worship and sacrifice at the temple in Jerusalem. Now returning home, he struggled with unanswered questions while reading a scroll of Isaiah's prophecy: *He was led like a sheep to the slaughter.* Who could this be?

Suddenly he was aware of someone alongside his chariot. "Do you understand what you're reading?" asked the stranger.

"How can I unless someone helps me make sense of it?" he replied, "If I give you a ride, will you tell me what it means?" Philip needed no second invitation to jump aboard.

Sometimes we sense that certain encounters take place by divine appointment. As the Ethiopian unburdened himself to Philip, the evangelist's mind was probably buzzing... "What if I hadn't come? What if I'd pretended not to hear? Lord, thank you ... thank you so much for the seemingly insignificant moment!"

The Ethiopian returned home, probably the only Christian in his country, for a short time at least. Philip, the risk-taker, had not simply led someone to Christ, but sown the seed of the Gospel in an entire nation.

There is always risk in physical danger

In Acts 9 we are introduced to another risk-taker called Ananias. He's a respectable, law-abiding citizen, still enjoying the "honeymoon" of his new relationship with God. The only blot on his horizon is an evil man named Saul. But he's still far away in Jerusalem and not an immediate threat.

Then God told Ananias to do the unthinkable and go look for Saul, a man notorious for searching out and persecuting Christians. No Christian ever went looking for him! Ananias could have disobeyed. And even if he risked obeying, it may be the last time he went where God was directing him.

He was baffled by God referring to Saul as "my chosen instrument" and may have even considered it a case of divine mistaken identity. As Ananias followed God's direction to walk down Straight Street toward the house of Judas, he may have been thinking, "It seems impossible to me, but I sincerely hope you're right, Lord!"

Taking a deep breath, he knocked on the door and was admitted. And there was his former enemy — the one whom he had prayed for, but always avoided. He was able to call him, "Brother Saul." And Saul, blind since his life-changing encounter on the Damascus Road, was relieved to meet the man sent by God to restore his sight and baptize him.

The obedience of Ananias that day planted seeds that blossomed into some of the greatest evangelistic activity across the ancient world as Saul became Paul the Apostle. But you know what? Ananias is never again mentioned in the New Testament. There aren't even churches dedicated to St. Ananias, the risk-taker. But his obedience was crucial to the growth of the Church, and the reason we are believers today.

There is risk in evangelism

The kingdom of God doesn't progress until his people are prepared to take risks. This is true in everything concerning the kingdom, especially in the realm of evangelism.

Jesus said to his disciples, *you will be my witnesses in Jerusalem, and in all Judea and Samaria, and to the ends of the earth* (Acts 1:8).

Where is my Jerusalem? Where do I feel comfortable, useful and unthreatened? There's nothing wrong with Jerusalem, but Jesus is unlikely to be satisfied with us simply being "at ease in Zion." He sees a potential harvest in Judea and Samaria. Who are the people I feel are not quite "kosher"? They probably strike me as all right in some ways, but at other times, I just don't feel comfortable around them.

The first Jewish believers didn't feel comfortable with Gentiles. Who are my Gentiles? Who are those people with whom I feel nothing in common, even those who make me thoroughly uncomfortable to be around? Their lifestyles are alien to mine. I can't ever imagine being friends with people like that, nor find any possible common ground.

The Acts of the Apostles continues to be written today. The Acts of Jesus have not stopped. He continues to press us, gently but firmly, into new areas of discomfort, growth and influence for the kingdom. We might as well give in graciously, and become risk-takers for him.

The Greeks had a word for it

The word "risky" is derived from the Greek *paraboleuothai*. It's a gambler's term meaning *to stake everything on the turn of the dice*.

In the days of the early church, there was a group of men and women called *the parabolani* – the gamblers. They visited prisoners and the sick, especially those afflicted with dangerous and infectious diseases.

In 252 AD, a plague broke out in Carthage, a city in North Africa, close to where the city of Tunis is today. The people of that city threw the dead bodies outside the walls, later fleeing the city in terror, leaving the sick and dying to perish on their own. Cyprian, the main pastor of that area, gathered his congregation together to bury the dead and nurse the sick back to health. The city was saved because they were willing to take a risk.

Today's church needs the *parabolani* – the gamblers, the risk-takers. While you may never have reason to visit someone with an infectious, and possibly fatal disease, or a political prisoner, you may face other risky situations.

Three things that may be risky, but worth it

It may be risky to speak

Some Christians tell me that one of their greatest fears is talking to someone about their faith in Jesus. What if they get offended? What if they make fun of me? What if they ask a question I cannot answer? What if it has a negative effect on our relationship?

Speaking can be risky. Risky, but worth it. If you're running a risk by speaking about Jesus, think of the other person. They're at greater risk if they don't hear the Good News.

Are you waiting for someone else to tell them? God places some people within our circle of influence that may never be reached by someone else. He's counting on us.

The chances are that most of us who have accepted Jesus, did so because someone took a risk to share the Gospel with us.

One of the last things Jesus said was: "Run the risk, tell everyone about me." Alright, those may not have been his exact words, but he did say, *preach the good news to all* (Mark 16:15), and often that involves taking a risk.

It may be risky to serve

When you accept that God calls us to be servants, first to him and then to others, you take an immense risk. Servants are not always appreciated. Sometimes people take advantage of them. And as you contemplate serving God and others, you may worry, "What if my own needs aren't met? If I just give myself to serving others, who is going to serve me?"

Many Christians don't want to get involved in ministry because they're afraid it will cut into their own needs.

"I don't want to get involved in the children's ministry, because I need to be in the service myself. How will I get fed otherwise?"

"I don't want to get involved in the youth ministry, because I need to relax after a hard day at the office."

"I don't want to get involved in the Saturday food outreach to the homeless, because that's my day off."

"I don't want to get involved in being an usher or greeter, because that means having to be at church earlier, and I need to sleep in on the weekends."

It's risky to serve, because sometimes your own needs may be put on hold. But something interesting happens when we decide to run the risk of serving. We soon discover that our needs *are* being met. God never short-changes us.

Jesus said that one of the greatest things Christians will hear from God when they stand before him is, *Well done, good and faithful servant.*

It may be risky to stand

It's risky to stand for what's right, what's true, and what's moral. Perhaps your boss wants you to lie, and you say you can't do that. That's risky. During a coffee break at work, the friends you're with are laughing at an off-color joke, and you don't. That's risky.

When you decide to stand against lying and cheating, to be a person of integrity who is faithful, trustworthy, and has high standards of morality, you run the risk of being rejected, made fun of and ridiculed. Sometimes when you take the risk of standing up for the truth, you may find that you're standing alone. But take courage! Share your faith! (Who knows, maybe someone will be drawn to Jesus.) Serve! (Who knows, maybe someone may be blessed.) Stand! (Who knows, maybe you'll be ridiculed.) But Jesus said *God blesses you when you are mocked and persecuted and lied about because you are my followers. Be happy about it! Be very glad! For a great reward awaits you in heaven…* (Matt 5:11-12).

It may be risky to speak, but it's worth it. It may be risky to serve, but it's worth it. It may be risky to stand, but it's worth it.

When Peter saw Jesus walking on the water, he leaped out of the boat to walk toward him. Where would Peter have been if he had not stepped out of the boat? Unlike the other disciples still in the boat, Peter experienced the power of Jesus who rescued him as he started to sink. Maybe God is asking us to step out of the boat of our comfort zones, and to trust him in new and exciting ways.

We need to be like Epaphroditus, like the *parabolani*, like Ruth, Jeremiah and Paul. Who knows what adventures await us when we are willing to be risk-takers for God?

Meet some of today's risk-takers

Through the years I've met many modern-day risk-takers. Here are just a few:

Karen is a wonderful southern lady who had never been on a plane, or even to an airport, before 2003. But she took the risk of flying across the Atlantic to minister to women and orphans in Bulgaria. She overcame what was to her a giant obstacle.

Susan is a young widow who flew to Ukraine, and then took a 20-hour train journey from the capital city of Kiev to Kerch, in Crimea. Her purpose? To minister to needy children. Because she took that risk, her life was so enriched that it will never be quite the same again.

Over the years, John was a successful businessman who worked and lived in many places around the world. Then, he sensed there was more to life than making money. Taking early retirement, he ventured out into full-time Christian service, encouraging other believers to see what God is doing outside America. Today he's a full-fledged risk-taker, leading teams of people to serve Christ around the world.

Bob was a businessman who decided to invest in God's kingdom instead of his own. During his 70 years of working in the family business, he literally gave away millions of dollars. Several million people around the world have been able to hear and respond to the Gospel because of Bob and his wife, Eleanor. Instead of spending most of it on themselves, they took the risk of investing in God's kingdom.

Remember, the greatest risk is not to risk at all. If you are not a risk-taker, you become a caretaker. And if you remain a caretaker for too long, you may eventually end up being the undertaker for the talents God gave you.

Some risks we can take for God

Most people don't even know their own neighbors. Befriend them by inviting them for a barbeque. Don't force the Gospel on them. Just take the opportunity to get to know them.

But be sensitive to God's Spirit in case he opens the door to share your faith. You may say, "You don't know my neighbors; with them the door is firmly shut!" Maybe, but closed doors are not always locked. They may simply be waiting for someone to turn the handle.

Invite a friend to your church, a Bible study or an Alpha course. There is a 50 percent chance they'll accept!

Pray for someone you don't really think the Lord can touch. It may be for salvation, for restoration of their marriage relationship, or even for healing. Take a risk and trust God to step in!

Find needs in your neighborhood. Perhaps a neighbor is in the hospital and the rest of the family needs help. Offer to give them a ride somewhere, to pick up some groceries, or invite them to a meal!

Invite neighbors for coffee. They may ask questions about the obviously well-used (and well-placed!) Bible on your coffee table. Even risk asking them to move it so you can put down the tray! It may be the first time they've held a Bible in a long time, if at all. You could even take the greater risk of commenting, "Oh, I haven't had time for my daily reading yet. Would you like to hear it? It happens to be one of my favorites, the third chapter of John!"

If this sounds far-fetched, I heard a story about some American Christians living in a Middle Eastern country who invited non-Christian neighbors to a Christmas celebration to give them a glimpse of how Americans celebrate the holiday. At the appropriate point, they said, "And this is when we read the Christmas story… and, by the way, so you can follow as we read in English, we managed to find New Testaments in your language." Later, when their guests were leaving, they said, "Do take the New Testaments with you because we can't read them."

Use your financial resources for the kingdom beyond what you ever thought possible. Plan for greater kingdom dividends by investing in Christian nationals. While there is still a need for traditional missionaries in some areas, nationals can be so much more effective in their own culture. They already know the language and the best way to approach their own people. What's more, they can usually be supported at a fraction of the cost of a missionary from another country.

Share your story of Jesus with someone. Tell them in three minutes who you were before you met Christ, how you met him, and the difference it made after he came into your life. They cannot argue with your personal experience. It's your story, and it's worth the risk!

Go on a mission trip somewhere in the world. People in Latin America, Eastern Europe, Western Europe, India and Africa are waiting for you. If you're like others I know, your first trip will not be your last. Chances are you'll make it a regular experience.

Encourage friends in your church to consider taking on a mission project, either locally, nationally or internationally.

Become a catalyst to take a risk for God in your church. Look for opportunities to live your Christian life outside of "the box." Encourage others to join you. Discover what it means for you personally to step out of your boat.

How effective are we believers in taking risks today?

Over the past years, I have been to more than 40 pastors' conferences, attended by more than 40,000 pastors. As I hear them talk, it seems effectiveness is measured by such criteria as:

- A full range of activity programs for everyone.
- A new building — or at least some kind of building program on the drawing board.

- A growing number of members and attendees.
- A budget that expands as attendance increases.

Just imagine if effectiveness was not even measured by people coming to Christ. What would happen if the health of the church was measured by the effectiveness of making disciples? Jesus said, *All authority in heaven and on earth has been given to me. Therefore go and make disciples of all nations, baptizing them in the name of the Father and of the Son and of the Holy Spirit, and teaching them to obey everything I have commanded you* (Matt 28:18-20).

Our primary purpose in taking risks for God is to "make disciples." And the only measurement for success is the quality and functionality of those disciples who, in turn, make other disciples. Today, that measurement of success is severely lacking in many churches.

Who did Jesus ask to become risk-takers?

He asked his disciples who were called by him then, just as you and I are called by him now. They became extremely passionate about serving him and that gave them a strong incentive to become risk-takers for God.

How many Christians do you know who have "making disciples" as their life purpose? How many believers wake up every morning, saying: "I can't wait to get out of bed to make some more disciples today!"

Discipleship is not about reading books and storing up knowledge. Disciples are learners who are in love with Jesus, and who have a passionate desire to please him. He is the master, and they are apprentices.

In the movie series *Star Wars*, one of the Jedi masters, Yoda, portrays this principle in his strange English, as he proclaims, "Two there always are... a master and an apprentice." The Jedi apprentice's sole desire is to become like his Jedi master. That is the essence of our Christian walk: to become like our master, Jesus Christ.

In his book, *Growing True Disciples,* George Barna writes:

...few churches have a church of disciples. Maybe that's because for many Christians today, including Christian leaders, disciple-ship is not terribly important. If we can get people to attend worship services, pay for the church's buildings and salaries, and muster positive, loving attitudes toward one another and toward the world, we often feel that's good enough.

But risk-takers are people completely sold out to Christ. Barna continues:

To what are you absolutely, fanatically devoted? Jesus did not minister, die, and rise from the dead merely to enlist fans. He gave everything he had to create a community of uncompro-mising zealots — raving, unequivocal, undeterrable, no-holds-barred, spiritual revolutionaries. He has no room for lukewarm followers. He is not interested in those who have titles, prestige and self-sufficiency. He's searching for the broken, hopeless, helpless, spiritually dependent individuals, who readily acknowl-edge that they cannot make any headway without total and ab-solute dependence on him.

He is seeking the hearts of those who are willing to surrender everything for the blessed privilege of suffering for him, just as he suffered for us. He wants people who are dedicated to getting beyond the offer of mere salvation — those who are willing to do what it takes to complete a personal transformation.

Discipleship is a lifelong calling that demands every resource we can muster, as we trust God for the strength we need. It is about a passion to reach our full potential in Jesus Christ, to step out of our boats and become risk-takers.

Where did he ask them to go?
Jesus sent his disciples to various parts of their world, simulta-neously to Judea, Samaria and the ends of the earth. Today, he has placed us just where he needs us, in our "Jerusalem." Are we

willing to risk being led further, to "Judea," "Samaria" or even the "ends of the earth"?

Some of us may only be able to go for a short-term mission trip, but we can also enable others to go by our prayers and by our financial support.

Recently I worked with a small church in Europe, assisting them in formulating their mission statement. I was amazed and thrilled when they suggested: We want to be a church with life and power that changes the world by influencing people to become followers of Jesus Christ. They wanted to be risk-takers!

What did he promise them?

Jesus promised to be with his disciples as they went out, with power beyond their own human resources. This promise still holds true for us, because Hebrews 13:8 assures us, *Jesus Christ is the same yesterday and today and forever.* And his relationship with 21st century disciples is the same as with those of the 1st century.

The problem is that we tend to sit and simply be recipients. He will bless us even in that sedentary position, but not to the extent that we experience when we take more risky steps for him. That's when we discover his presence in the very power that raised him from the dead!

Dutch holocaust survivor and evangelist Corrie ten Boom once said, "When Jesus calls us to walk a rough road, he gives us strong shoes."

What happens when you become a risk-taker for God?

When you take risks, people's lives change! Communities can be transformed when enough people within them are changed. Society is shaken when a church is true to God's Word and to his commands. In some parts of the world, I've seen that lead to persecution. But don't be deterred by that, because I've never seen a persecuted believer who expressed regret at being a risk-taker for God. I've even met pastors in areas of intense pressure who smile and say, "They think the worst thing they can do is kill me, but that's not so. The worst thing they can possibly do is dilute my devotion to God."

We cannot help but have a positive impact on the world when we are being Christ-like, but we will not be loved and accepted by everyone.

God is calling us to become risk-takers for him, within our own spheres of influence... in our home, to our wider family, friends and neighbors, to those with whom we work, and perhaps to those who serve or work for us.

The major hindrance to the advancement of the Gospel today is not money, resources, equipment or even properties from which to minister. As someone once said, "The heart of the problem is the problem of the heart"... my heart and your heart. But when we allow God to touch our hearts, he creates a willingness within us to take risks for him!

Jesus risked everything for us. You can also become a risk-taker!

CHAPTER TWENTY-TWO
YOU CAN start over

In my years as an evangelist, I often prayed with people who had come into the prayer room, or, during the summers, into the prayer tent. Many of those people I counseled were under desperate conviction. Quite a few of them sensed that their lives had fallen completely apart.

"We had such a great marriage, but then my husband left me. To dull the pain, I began taking drugs. Then, my children abandoned their druggie mother, and there was nothing left except thoughts of suicide. Where do I turn? There is no hope for me."

"I was training for ministry, and all was going seemingly well. Except, I had this one enormous temptation in my life. Every day, I had to satisfy my need for pornography. I would sneak out and buy magazines and rent videos. Finally I was caught and told to leave the Bible College. I drifted into the arms of prostitutes and life just fell apart. Is there any way to start afresh?"

"We had an argument on the elder board. I lost my temper and stomped out of the meeting, slamming the door. That was ten years ago. My wife and I never returned to that church. Our friends disowned us. Bitterness over those issues festered until all my emotions were completely spent, and I became hard as a rock inside. Tonight, God's Spirit penetrated my heart. Is there any way to put back together what fell to pieces so long ago?"

None of those situations may reflect yours today. However, you may feel as if everything has fallen apart. You may be dealing with old, painful secret sins, marriage issues, perhaps being forgotten by your own children, or even life itself. Have you ever looked at your circumstances and thought, *I would love to have a chance to relive that differently?* Or *If I could just change that, I would. I need a fresh start.*

John chapter 8 tells the story of a woman caught in adultery. The Jewish law declared that marital unfaithfulness was punishable by stoning. Religious leaders brought the woman to Jesus to see if he would follow the Law of Moses and condemn her to death. But to their surprise, Jesus did not accuse her. After writing on the ground, Jesus said, *He who is without sin among you, let him be the first to throw a stone at her* (John 8:7). The group slowly dispersed, the oldest ones leaving first.

After all of them had gone, Jesus looked at the woman. She understood he was a man of God. How exposed and embarrassed she must have felt! Then Jesus spoke to her about forgiveness and gave an opportunity for her to start over. *I do not condemn you ... Go. From now on sin no more* (John 8:11). He forgave the woman and set her free.

Maybe at one point in your life you had big dreams. You were going to go places. You wanted a huge house, a nice job, the perfect husband or wife, and a handful of perfectly behaved children. Instead, you were fired from your job, your husband (or wife) left you for another soul mate, and the children messed with drugs and are in a juvenile center. You could not pay the mortgage so they repossessed your house, and you are living in a sparsely-furnished one-room apartment. Every night you lay awake and wonder: *Why is my life like this? What do I live for? Why do I fight these battles anymore?* The only conclusion you arrive at is utter hopelessness. Today, many people are simply empty shells of brokenness. They paste a smile on their faces, and laugh their way through life, or maybe they become depressed and withdraw from it all. Suicides occur every day at unprecedented rates. Where is the hope? Where is the peace? Where is the purpose and meaning for life here in the real world?

Maybe you feel like you have messed up too many times. You may think that God can never forgive you now. You have gone too far. You think it may be too late.

Jesus wants to start over with you

One of my favorite Scriptures is found in Jeremiah 18:1-6.

The LORD gave another message to Jeremiah. He said, 'Go down to the potter's shop, and I will speak to you there.' So I did as he told me and found the potter working at his wheel. But the jar he was making did not turn out as he had hoped, so he crushed it into a lump of clay again and started over. Then the LORD gave me this message: 'O Israel, can I not do to you as this potter has done to his clay? As the clay is in the potter's hand, so are you in my hand.'

It does not matter how broken up your life may be. It does not matter what you have done, or where you have been. The Master of all potters wants to mend your broken vessel. He has provided a "put it back together" plan for your life. He doesn't care what you have done, or the mess you have made. He wants to make you whole again. Jesus Christ gave his life on the cross for our salvation. When you think of your sins, and how much you owe the Lord, in despair you may say, "Who can pay such a debt?" Whisper the name of Jesus. He can pay it. In fact, Jesus paid it all. God gave his own son so he could come and collect the broken pieces of your life. He loved you enough that he gave his own blood to mend your broken clay plot.

He doesn't throw the clay away. He reshapes it. When everyone else says you are worth nothing, he takes the pieces, just as a potter would. He molds the pieces together to a new lump of clay, one without scars or brokenness. He reformats the failures of your life into a new vessel that looks beautiful in his eyes. Suddenly your clay pot is turned into something worthwhile and valuable.

God is an expert in using broken things. A lady came to Jesus with some oil. The neck of the bottle had to be broken so the oil could flow. On the night before Jesus was betrayed, he took bread and broke it, saying, *this is the body that is broken for you.* The next day, his own body was broken on the cross for you and me. He can use things that are broken. He can use you again.

There is an old Swedish song that has meant so much to me when I sensed that my life had smashed in pieces, as a clay plot would when it falls to the floor. The song is not available in English but the gist of the song is this.

> In the hand of my Master are pieces of clay
> From a vessel that failed to take shape
> His heart cries in pain, as it's obvious to him
> Of expectations, nothing remains
> But because of his love he starts over again
> Molding clay to reflect his own will
> As he shapes me again, his hope is fulfilled
> A vessel that's worthy of him

Chorus:

> Oh, start over again in my life
> Oh, start over again in my life
> Reshape me anew, by the power of your Word
> Make my life to be a tool in your hand

> Make me willing to be like clay in his hand
> To be holy, transparent and pure
> My life I commit to his service today
> As long as I am living on earth
> In his hands I am resting, fully aware
> He's not finished shaping the frail clay
> Till it's molded by him for life here on earth
> To the shape that reflects his own heart

Do you feel like a broken piece of pottery? God has come to reshape your vessel. When everyone else says that you are worthless, God says you are worth everything. He wants to take the broken pieces of your life and reshape them into something new. He can take the worst of homes and make them peaceful. He can take the worst of addicts and make them clean. He can take the hottest temper and cool it to reflect his Spirit. He can change the thirst of the most intense alcoholic. He can take a wrecked marriage and put it back together again. What makes us think he can't remake our lives?

Not only does God want to remake your vessel, but he wants to fill it until it flows over. That emptiness that you have felt, God desires to fill. The lonely worthlessness, he wants to fill. God desires to come inside your heart and fill it with what has been missing. He doesn't just want to buy your vessel, and repair it, and keep it as a nice keepsake to place on a shelf, but he wants to fill you to overflowing with his Spirit so that you can be used by him.

He can start over with you, so you can start over with him.

CHAPTER TWENTY-THREE
YOU CAN change the world

I alone cannot change the world,
But I can cast a stone across the waters
To create many ripples

                    Mother Teresa

When we look at the world, it is so huge. Imagine approximately seven billion inhabitants with at least five problems each. That makes a lot of problems. It is easy to give up and say, "Why does it matter what I do?"

One day while visiting Kolkata many years ago, I was completely overwhelmed. How could a loving and kind God send all these masses to eternal separation from him, when they had not really heard about him? How could God forgive a church who had heard about him but did not seem to care about those who had not? Which sin was the greatest? How would he deal with it?

That morning, we visited the railway station in the heart of Kolkata to evaluate a program among street people in the slums, in an attempt to figure out how to get Scriptures to them. The station was so crowded you had to press yourself in between people to move forward. There were kids begging, stealing, accosting you for every possible service they could provide wherever you turned, including polishing your shoes while you were trying to walk!

Finally, I could not take it anymore and we grabbed a cab to return to the hotel. Sitting in my hotel room, I argued with God. Was there really any hope? Did it matter one iota what I did or did not do? Why was I trying to kill myself with so much hard work?

Why was I away from my family two-thirds of the year — if it did not really matter?

Late that afternoon, we had tea with an elderly lady in Kolkata, and I was sharing some of my frustrations with her. She took my hand in hers and looked me straight in the eye. "Dr. Lars, don't be frustrated! People are born one at a time, live one at a time and die one at a time — and you share the love of Jesus with them, one at a time!" Mother Theresa's words to me that afternoon are still an encouragement when I feel overwhelmed and frustrated.

There were other times I simply did not, and still do not feel, capable of completing the task the Lord and other responsible people have placed on my shoulders. How can I, a Swede with a language complex and very little formal education in business or theology, make this work successful? Has the lack of funds made me incapable of running an organization the way I should have done? I have turned away many projects and people throughout the years, simply because of a lack of resources. While at times I trust people too much, and am slow to let people go, I have turned down more projects than I have accepted. And the truth that I am not a Harvard MBA graduate, but only a "simple" evangelist from a minority country has always haunted me.

As I matured in my faith, I knew I could not do it all. But I had to overcome my shyness and being such an introvert. The needs of the world are still so overwhelming to me. But one thing I do know. I want to throw as many stones as I am capable of across the waters and create as many ripples as possible. What about you?

What is the problem with the world?

As long as the world has been in existence, people have tried to solve its problems. Some have tried conquering other nations by war, an art that has never made much sense to me. Others have tried to improve the world through diplomacy. Some believe that if we had a better economic plan for the world, everyone would live in peace. Yet others insist that education for all will solve all the major problems in the world. "If we could only eradicate poverty," they say, "then people would live in peace and the world's problems would be solved."

The real problem is not financial, educational or diplomatic. The real problem lies within the human heart. We can have the most educated thieves, the most financially savvy people deceiving people out of their savings, or politicians hoarding food as a political weapon.

The world is really in bondage to the human heart. Have we ever really understood that Jesus is the only answer to every problem in every country, as well as this country? He is the answer to every problem in your city. He is the answer to every person's problem in your city, and of course to yours as well. Jesus said: *The Spirit of the Lord is upon me for he has anointed me to bring Good News to the poor. He has sent me to proclaim that captives will be released, that the blind will see, that the oppressed will be set free, and that the time of the Lord's favor has come* (Luke 4:18-19).

Jesus is the same, today, yesterday and forever. When Jesus was twelve years old, he said to his parents, when they found him in the temple with the professors of theology and law of those days: *Did you not know that I must be about My Father's business?* (Luke 2:49). Some translations say *I must be about my Father's affairs.*

> *Again Jesus said, Peace be with you! As the Father has sent me, I am sending you.* (John 20:21).

Are you willing to be about his affairs and do what he asks you to do, and go where he wants you to go?

We have the good news

Each morning my alarm clock radio goes off. Sometimes, it is just as the news begins, and the voice says, "Good morning, here's the news." Most days the news is not great. News reporters describe plane crashes, bomb explosions, murder and rape. This world is just full of bad news.

Today is the day for good news as far as believers are concerned. However, for some reason, we keep silent.

Look at the people around you. Many of their lives are in a mess. They seem to be running from one garbage heap to another. We don't have to tell them how bad they are. But we can tell them, *taste and see that the Lord is good.* If we do that every day, the Gospel will spread rapidly and the world will be transformed.

We are his ambassadors

When I was ten years old, a huge passenger cruise ship came into Stockholm. It was so large, it could not even dock, but little boats ferried the passengers to the quay where I was standing, watching, and leaning on my bicycle. The people that came off those little boats amazed me. I had never seen people like that before. This was the mid-1950s, and the men wore plaid pants, large cowboy hats, and had the biggest cameras I had ever seen on straps around their necks. They spoke a language I didn't understand. The ladies wore gym shoes, lots of makeup and seemed to have blue-rinsed hair. All I remembered was that they were loud. Someone told me these people were Americans. To me, they were the ambassadors from their country.

Many years later, Doreen and I were on a ferry between Denmark and Sweden. There was a gang of Swedish young people making an awful lot of noise. They were completely drunk, falling over each other, and vomiting. They were not good ambassadors for my country.

Today, you and I are ambassadors for Christ's kingdom. Acts 1:8 explains it well. *But you will receive power when the Holy Spirit comes upon you. And you will be my witnesses, telling people about me everywhere – in Jerusalem, throughout Judea, in Samaria, and to the ends of the earth.*

As God's ambassador, you are part of "Plan A" in God's way to reach the world. He has called the individuals in each church to be ambassadors for him. He could probably have called 10,000 angels, but instead he chose us. He doesn't even have a Plan B.

You are a unique person. He wants to use your personality, gifts, abilities, and talents. You are called to be God's spokesperson.

One day God will say to us: "Well done you good and faithful ambassador. I led you to a group of people who desperately needed you; your personality, your sense of humor, your age factor, and your life. I commissioned you to go to them and you were a faithful spokesperson. Well done."

Every day, I wonder what situation God will bring my way so that I can be his ambassador to the people I meet.

There is no greater joy than leading a person to Christ

Fifteen years after I left my responsibilities for Youth for Christ in Britain, I attended a worldwide YFC convocation in Hong Kong. One morning, I stepped into the elevator in the high rise hotel to go down for breakfast. Uncomfortably, I noticed the only other occupant of the elevator, a Western man, eying me up and down. Suddenly, he addressed me, "You are Lars Dunberg, aren't you?" I nodded. "I can't believe how fat you have become," he said with a smile. I beckoned him to sit down with me in the lobby, and he told his story.

"Last time I met you, you were as thin as a rake. It was at a YFC rally in Loughton... do you remember that night?" Yes, I did remember that night of failure. The hall was like a shoebox, standing on its side. The hall was dimly lit. There was only a small audience, all of them sitting two-thirds down the hall. A lady sang a solo before I preached. She should never have attempted to sing in public. As I went on stage to preach, I realized the stage was very much higher than the audience, and this alienated me even more from the people in front of me. It was hard to speak. Every word became like a glass bubble that crashed to the floor far below me. I went home that night and told my wife, "I will never preach again!"

I had no memory of the young man sitting in front of me now. He continued, "That night, I sat in that audience and you preached the Gospel, which I heard for the first time. Later that night, as I returned home, I invited Jesus to come into my life." Bob continued to share with me how he had become involved in youth work through YFC, literally ministering to thousands of kids in Europe. Even a failed presentation can lead people to Christ!

Imagine, just one time, have one person look you in the eye, and tell you, "I was on the road heading for hell, and God used you to bring me to himself. Jesus saved me, but you led me to the cross!" What a joy. "I needed an ambassador from Jesus, and it was you."

Jesus is about his Father's affairs. He invites you to be about his Father's affairs. Think of 2-3 things that are hindering you from doing his will. Then, pray to God to remove them, give you power to go through them, and ask his Holy Spirit to equip you.

He uses the most ordinary people to do the impossible.

You may say, "I wish I was an extraordinary person, with a degree in theology, and a way to express myself. But I am just an ordinary person, and I am not sure that God can use me. I'm not sure he even wants to."

Let me tell you about three very different people I met in 2011, in Honduras. They were all attending a training course for pastors or prospective pastors. They looked like the most unlikely pastoral candidates I could have imagined. Two of them were men, and one was a woman. Here are their stories.

From gang-leader to evangelist

At the age of twenty-two, Mauricio Flores became the leader of a gang in Honduras. A major drug addict, he always dressed in black and began to tattoo his entire body. Mauricio terrorized his neighborhood and committed the most horrible crimes you can imagine. "I was vile and evil," explains Mauricio. "I stole from my parents to buy drugs, which was so sad, because they were hard working people." He left home and used to spend his nights sleeping under a bridge. He described himself as the most bitter and unhappy person in the world.

One day, while Mauricio was alone and very high on drugs, he heard a voice that told him to look at all his tattoos. He started looking at the ones on his feet and legs and worked his way up to his upper body. As he looked at the ones on his right shoulder, he saw a vision. He noticed that he was not in his neighborhood anymore, but somewhere else. Then he saw two ways: one that had a sign that read, PENITENTIARY and another one that read, THE CHURCH OF JESUS CHRIST.

The "Voice" began to show him where he would end up if he continued doing the evil things he had done up until then. The "Voice" clearly told him that he would die in prison. Then the "Voice" said, "I hope you will choose the second way, because I will be waiting there for you." He immediately told the "Voice" that he had chosen the second way. At that moment, the vision was gone.

Mauricio showered for the first time in many days, cut his hair and went home to tell his mother that he was on his way to church. He asked her for one *Lempira* (about a nickel) to have something to give when they passed the offering plate. However, he ended up buying a cigarette with the money! The people at church let him come in only because they were afraid of him and of what he might do to them. "I know that it was not love they felt for me, but fear," Mauricio commented. That night, he gave his life to Christ, and God began his transformation. His entire family came to Jesus because of his testimony.

Right away, he began witnessing to other gang members and became the pastor of his first church. For the past four years, Mauricio has been in charge of a rehabilitation center for gang members and drug addicts, called "Hands of Mercy," where hundreds of people hear the message of Jesus Christ every day. He has raised ten leaders out of these hundreds who have come to Christ and those ten are now working full-time at ten different churches throughout the city. His hope is to enroll them in the same pastoral training program in a year or two.

From brothel madam to pastor!

Rosa Miriam Rodriguez was first driven into a promiscuous life-style when she found that her husband was cheating on her with her best friend. Her anger drove her to prostitution, and it did not take long before she was the owner of three brothels in Puerto Cortes, Honduras, the largest and most important seaport in Central America.

"Simply put," Rosa stated, "I was not only a prostitute, but also the owner and boss — the Madam." Rosa sold drugs and used them regularly herself, as well as alcohol. In this environment, she raised two children, a boy and a girl, who later became involved in gangs and drugs. She practiced witchcraft and during those rituals she was extremely promiscuous. Unknowingly, she had sex with three different men, who, before they died, made the confession to her that they had AIDS. It was a miracle that she never tested HIV-positive.

Rosa was the accomplice of seven murders of premature babies by performing abortions up until full-term gestation. Two of these babies were her own grandchildren. As the mothers were giving birth to the babies, she strangled them to death. "I was the lowest of the low" Rosa explains with sadness. It was when her seventeen-year-old daughter left home to become part of a gang and was later killed by her gang member boyfriend that she fell into a deep depression.

Her son was a drug addict, and in her desperation she looked for help at a well-known Christian rehabilitation center in the capital of Honduras, Tegucigalpa. It was at the center that Rosa heard the message of the Gospel for the first time. She left her son at the rehabilitation center and returned to her regular business activities. Waiting for her at her return, was a Christian lady who started visiting her at the brothels and fully explained the redeeming message of the Gospel to Rosa. During one of those visits, she gave her life to Jesus.

She closed down all her businesses and was discipled by her Christian friend. At that time, her son came out of the rehabilitation center with Jesus in his heart, but later was gunned down by drug traffickers, his former "friends."

"I had no idea how God could use someone like me," Rosa comments, "but I just had a passion to share the Gospel with everyone I came in contact with." Today, she has pastored a church for the past ten years, with approximately one hundred members, and she also operates ten home churches with some former prostitutes as members. She uses the home church model as the former prostitutes are generally rejected in a regular church environment.

"I didn't know if I was going to be able to keep up with the pastoral studies with only a fifth grade education, but from the first class, I have finally understood my true identity in Jesus Christ. I don't care when I hear people say, 'but wasn't she a prostitute?' I know what I was before and who I am now. I wait with anticipation for my next class, and every month God reveals himself to me like never before. Every month I gain more knowledge of the word, wisdom, and more importantly, I now have a true foundation of my faith that I can share with others, lost sinners, just as I was." Today, Rosa Miriam is planting churches in the country of Ecuador.

When a prostitute washed the feet of Jesus in Simon's house, Jesus said to him, *I tell you, her sins – and they are many – have been forgiven, so she has shown me much love. But a person who is forgiven little shows only little love. Then Jesus said to the woman, 'Your sins are forgiven'* (Luke 7:47-48).

Warden operates church in jail

The third person in the group sat there in full uniform, looking like a high level police officer. He was obviously a man of high importance, as I noticed what I call the "scrambled eggs" on his epaulettes and the peak of his uniform cap. Later I found out that his name was Junior Escalon. He shared this story with me.

"I am one of the wardens in the local jail. For several years, I have served in jails across the country, and God has used me to bring peace to some of the most troubled prisons throughout the country. Here in San Pedro Sula, I run a church among the inmates. Many of them have come to Christ." Later, Mr. Escalon was able to open the door for a pastoral training program in his jail, and the next year the first 13 pastors and leaders graduated inside the prison. He attended the graduation wearing a bulletproof vest, and surrounded by security guards, but his presence sent a clear message that God had given favor in that place.

***

Which people were most impacted by Jesus' ministry when he walked here on earth? There were not too many religious leaders or doctors of theology close to Jesus. However, the ones that were often touched by his ministry were the criminals, the prostitutes and the Roman officers. The Gospel has not changed!

Jesus wants us to develop a passion for his affairs

You will never move forward unless there is a passion driving you, and when you are gone, you will only be remembered for your passion. Today, we think of Henry Ford and his passion to give as many people as possible a car; Thomas Edison and his passion for inventions which gave us eventually the electric light. When we hear the name Mahatma Gandhi, we think of his passion for civil rights and freedom. Billy Graham, on the other hand, makes us think of his enormous passion for evangelism.

Jesus had a passion for his mission and goal in life: *For the son of man has come to seek and save that which is lost* (Luke 19:10). The passion of Jesus took him to the cross. Despite the pain and the suffering, he was obsessed with his passion.

Do you hate going to work? To church? Hoping the day will be over? Looking at the clock? Not having much success? Find out what your passion is! Look at Jesus and imitate him. Let your passion be for people and for the possibility of introducing them to Jesus, so that they can have their lives transformed, just as you have.

Jesus lived to save what was lost. His message, which started with a handful of followers after the resurrection, began to explode after the Day of Pentecost. Within the next few hundred years, the disciples and their followers had turned the world upside down with the Gospel.

You can also change the world. Introduce him to others, and you will soon notice how their lives are being changed, one at a time. He changed the world. And in his power, you can too.

Bibliography

Batterson, Mark. *Draw the Circle.* Grand Rapids: Zondervan, 2012.

Batterson, Mark. *The Circle Maker.* Grand Rapids: Zondervan, 2011.

Batterson, Mark. *Soul Print.* Colorado Springs: Multnomah, 2011.

Bounds, E.M. *The Weapon of Prayer.*
Grand Rapids: Baker Book House, 1931.

Bounds E.M. *The Possibilities of Prayer.*
Grand Rapids: Baker Book House, 1979.

Chan, Francis. *Crazy Love.* Colorado Springs: D. C. Cook, 2008.

Cymbala, Jim. *Breakthrough Prayer.* Grand Rapids: Zondervan, 2003.

Cymbala, Jim. *Spirit Rising.* Grand Rapids: Zondervan, 2012.

Cymbala, Jim. *You were made for more.* Grand Rapids: Zondervan, 2008.

Dunberg, Lars. *Becoming a Risk-taker.*
Colorado Springs, Global Action, 2003.

Dunberg, Lars. *Mentoring Risk-takers.*
Colorado Springs, Global Action, 2004.

Dunberg, Lars. *We Started a Church.*
Colorado Springs: Global Action, 2011.

Dunberg, Lars. *Risk-taker for God.*
Colorado Springs: Global Action, 2008.

Foster, Richard. *Prayer.* London: Hodder & Stoughton, 1992.

Green, Michael. *Evangelism for Amateurs.*
London: Hodder & Stoughton, 1998.

Green, Michael. *You must be Joking.* Hodder & Stoughton, 1976.

Gumbel, Nicky. *The Heart for Revival.*
Eastbourne: Kingsway Publications, 1997.

Gumbel, Nicky. *Questions of Life.*
Colorado Springs: David C. Cook, 2002.

Hybels, Bill. *Too Busy Not to Pray.*
Downers Grove: Intervarsity Press, 1988.

Idleman, Kyle. *Not a Fan.* Grand Rapids: Zondervan, 2011.

Little, Paul. E. *How to give away your faith.*
Downers Grove: Intervarsity Press, 1966.

Bibliography, cont.

McPhee, Arthur. *Friendship Evangelism.*
Eastbourne: Kingsway Publications, 1978.

Orr, J. Edwin. *Evangelical Awakenings in Southern Asia.*
Minneapolis: Bethany Fellowship, 1975.

Orr, J. Edwin. *The Church Must First Repent.* Public Domain, 1937.

Ortiz, Juan Carlos. *Call to Discipleship.*
Plainfield: Logos International, 1975.

Pippert, Rebecca Manley. *Out of the Saltshaker & into the World.*
Downers Grove: Intervarsity Press, 1979.

Plantinga, Cornelius Jr. *Not the way it's supposed to be – A Breviary of Sin.*
Grand Rapids: Eerdmans, 1995.

Platt, David. *Radical.* Colorado Springs: Multnomah, 2010.

Platt, David. *Radical together.* Colorado Springs: Multnomah, 2011.

Pudaite, Rochunga. *My Billion Bible Dream.*
Nashville: Thomas Nelson, 1982.

Ravenhill, Leonard. *Revival Praying.*
Minneapolis: Bethany House Publishers, 1962.

Stott, John R.W. *Baptism and Fullness: The Work of the Holy Spirit Today.*
Westmont: Inter-Varsity Press, 1976.

Taylor, Kenneth. N. *My Life a Guided Tour.*
Wheaton: Tyndale House Publishers, 1991.

Yancey, Philip D. *Prayer – Does it make any difference?*
Grand Rapids: Zondervan, 2006.

A variety of articles from Google on most subjects in this book.

Bring the warmth and challenge of
<u>You Can Change the World</u>
to your friends and family.

Simply use the enclosed cards. One will allow you to send a *free* hard copy of this book to a friend or family member. The other gives you a deep discount for buying multiple copies for small groups or even your church!

If the cards are missing from this book, please call (719) 323-2222 to receive this special offer.

> *"When we read the four Gospels we notice that five times Jesus says, 'Believe in me.' However, about twenty times he says, 'Follow me.' One is not more important than the other. But they cannot exclude each other."*
>
> — Lars Dunberg, <u>You Can Change the World</u>

You Can
Change the World
(and your life)
On a ServeNow
Mission Journey.

www.weservenow.org

The response: SERVE

The time: Now

ServeNow

procrastinate later

www.weservenow.org

You Can Turbocharge Your Local Church Outreach with Vital Volunteers.

SERVENOW ACTION PARTNERS
WWW.WESERVENOW.ORG / SNAP

YOU CAN HELP SPARE CHANGE SPARE LIVES.

Join us in saving hundreds of lives each year in Jesus'
name through this simple ServeNow program —
suitable for all ages!

Find out more by emailing
Change4Change@weservenow.org.

YOU CAN GIVE LOCAL CHURCHES THE PRACTICAL HELP THEY NEED NOW TO SERVE THEIR COMMUNITIES.

BE A SERVENOW SUSTAINER.

Some need Bibles. Some need warm clothing and blankets. Others need building repairs. Still others need help caring for young victims of human trafficking, or AIDS. Your monthly gift as a ServeNow Sustainer supports very practical responses to very practical needs that hundreds of churches submit to us each month. Faithful giving from people like you allows ServeNow to meet real needs of church partners in the heart of impoverished communities in Africa, Asia, Europe and North America quickly and efficiently.

Please take the time now to find out more about becoming a ServeNow Sustainer at www.weservenow.org. Your monthly gift could make a huge difference!

10 Prescriptions for a Somewhat Sick Church

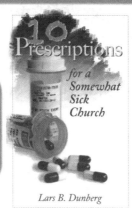

Lars B. Dunberg

Have you ever left church after a Sunday morning service and felt uneasy?

As much as you love your church, your pastor and your fellow believers, you can't help feeling that something is wrong?

You can't put your finger on it, but it bothers you, and it leaves you both uncomfortable and concerned.

Ten Prescriptions for a Somewhat Sick Church was written to identify some of those issues, but also to find and suggest remedies which will help the church to become all it was meant to be.

MOUNTAINBROOK

Order now at www.mountainbrookpress.com or call 719-323-2217

KNOW YOUR BASICS....

The Basic Things Series was created to provide an overview of the key concepts of the Christian faith. The title says it all: these are the basic things you need to know. A deep foundation is important if we are to build high, and a good understanding of the basics is crucial if we are to grow spiritually.

The Basic Things You Need to Know About Jesus, features Jesus Christ – his life, his teaching, and what he did and still does for each one of us.

The Basic Things You Need to Know About Reading and Studying The Bible was written to help you find the treasures that are within the pages of God's Word. You will be encouraged, blessed, and at times, challenged.

Order now at www.mountainbrookpress.com or call 719-323-2217
Check website for more of the *Basic Things* series.

TRUE FREEDOM STARTS
IN THE MIND

This book invites us to take thirty days to let God change our minds. He does it by gently replacing old, less helpful thought patterns with new, good and creative ones that only he can give. God spoke the universe into existence, and his words still have creative power. If we let God's words do their work, our lives will be changed. When our minds accept his ideas, we can truly rise above our chains.

Order now at www.mountainbrookpress.com or call 719-323-2217